WEAVE

WEAVE
NEW AND SELECTED POEMS

WENDY BARKER

Foreword by Alicia Ostriker

BkMk Press
Kansas City, Missouri

BkMk Press, Inc.
www.bkmkpress.org
Fine books since 1971

Cover photo and design: Cynthia Beard
Editor: Ben Furnish

Lbrary of Congress Cataloging-in-Publication data

Names: Barker, Wendy, author.
Title: Weave : new and selected poems / Wendy Barker.
Description: Kansas City, Missouri : BkMk Press, 2022 | Summary: "Weave:
   New and Selected Poems showcases poems from Barker's long career that
includes selections from her seven previous full-length collections, as well
as new work. The collection features a wide range of subjects and themes,
notable among them the poet's perspectives as an educator (especially in the
English-literature classroom), her family's stories, and her perspectives on
contemporary American life"-- Provided by publisher.
Identifiers: LCCN 2022048103 | ISBN 9781943491391 (trade paperback)
Classification: LCC PS3552.A67124 W43 2023 | DDC 811/.54--dc23
LC record available at https://lccn.loc.gov/2022048103

ISBN 978-1-943491-39-1

Weave is set in Gill Sans and Adobe Garamond Pro.

CONTENTS

from **THINGS OF THE WEATHER** (2008)

from **BETWEEN FRAMES** (2006)

from **POEMS FROM PARADISE** (2005)

from **WAY OF WHITENESS** (2000)

from **LET THE ICE SPEAK** (1991)

from **WINTER CHICKENS** (1990)

FOREWORD

Early in Wendy Barker's *Weave* we find the eyebrow-lifting title "On Salt." It begins like this:

> Neruda says the salt sings. But how about
>   Lot's wife, turned into salt for looking back? I can't
>   imagine she was singing. Maybe she turned her own
> self into salt, so she'd never forget
>   the kitchen where she simmered lentil stew,
>   he bed where she suckled her babies . . . .

We encounter, in this opening, a sensibility whose light, conversational touch gathers together ancient and modern cultures, contradiction, curiosity and whim, and the serious business of being a woman unashamed by what the female body is and does, even unto death. A bit later in this poem, in the midst of grieving a friend lost to cancer, the poet wonders if salt from tears "could harden to a stone pillar," wishes she could erase the memory of moments of humiliation,

>   moments when I've been bullied, flattened
>   by comments that sliced through my skin. At times
> these tauntings attack me in dreams
>   like salt stinging a wound. Before refrigeration,
>   salt kept fish and pork flesh from decay, preserved
> our food. Easy to know when to dump
>   rotten meat, that stink. But not so easy to know
>   when or how to dump a memory.

The hairpin turn from psychic hurt to "refrigeration," associated with comfort and modernity but also with pain and self-protection—that never descends to self-pity—and the almost unnoticed shift from first-person singular "I" to the general case of "our" food, is typical. The poet is glad to remember her toddler son's "little chuckle." "But if we remember too much, we might be / paralyzed, turned into a salty rock-hard / column." I wondered, as I was reading this variations-on-a-theme poem, whether it was a poem of anger or of sorrow, and concluded it was both. It is certainly a poem about the human need to remember and to forget. Swinging easily from the individual "I" to the universal "we," it turns in the end to something larger than either "I" or "we":

> Neruda says the salt plain near Antofagasta is singing
> of grief. That entire plain, I've read, is ringed
>   by mountains and volcanos, cone-shaped, composed
>   of hardened lava and ash, some of them active, alive.

Barker herself is active and alive. From her earliest poems written in the 1970s and 1980s to her most recent work, she responds to the world around her, and the world within her, with attentive warmth. Family and domesticity dominate her first books, punctuated by loopholes to what lies beyond. In "Father's Fish," we can see the poet's father fishing as a kind of stealth ars poetica. In "Winter Chickens," after "red wattles hang from their heads, / eggs squirm through swollen vents," we follow the fate of the eggs being poached or scrambled, "sliding around like shoes on mud," and conclude with a jolt, "the shells go back to the hens, / grit for their old, hard beaks." There is something keenly anthropological about Barker's gaze here, beyond good and evil. A child's game of Statues links to Michelangelo's "Four slaves…still trying to separate / sinewy arms from the bulk of marble." Reading this, I think what a good word "bulk" is, and how children frozen in that game are in fact busy separating themselves from the bulk of family and the past. The poet presses language into the task of capturing exactly what is going on deep down and on the surface of things.

In subsequent collections Barker continues to turn her attentive gaze upon external and internal phenomena as mutually reflective, with a scrupulous tracking of the subtleties of human feeling. Some of these books focus on very specific aspects of the poet's history. A bravura set of meditations on color in *From the Moon, Earth Is Blue* rides easily from brown, "Least glamorous of pigments, / the impressionists got rid of it," to the grey of a mother's ashes, and then a kind of reeling ecstasy facing an Ellsworth Kelly painting. Shimmer fuses esthetics, affection, and embarrassment regarding the expensive family silver she has inherited. She makes you know that she admires the design and weight of these things. She also makes you know that she is ruefully aware of her state of privilege in owning them. Gloss extends these meditations on family history and family possessions, with their posh and poverty, to family secrets layered as the rocks of the Grand Canyon, in another brilliant evocation of timeless geology:

> And who would want
> to mend that great magenta-, purple-, blood-shaded tip in the earth's
> surface? It's what we come for,
> to gawk at all those layers, exposed.

Personal history is layered as firmly, and as delicately, everywhere. The prose poems of Nothing Between Us, published in 2009, recount a stint in the Sixties teaching in a half-black high school where she learns not to say "folks" to the kids, has a gratifying affair with a black gym teacher, and is radiantly, touchingly, young. One Blackbird at a Time gives us an older Barker, teaching literature and creative writing in a university where she is, as I have noted elsewhere, "the prof who can't help embracing literature, students, and life—sensuous, cruel, funny, generous, outrageous, personal." These are some of her very best poems, anecdotal and analytical at once, free-associating like a deer leaping through woods, like a cellist leaning to her task. I enjoy the comedy of "I Hate Telling People I Teach English," and the way it ends with a dentist reciting The Prologue of Chaucer's Canterbury Tales, but also the way a class discussion of Passage to India leads to a self-examination on the topics of colonialism and rape, while a discussion of Mrs. Dalloway makes it clear that nobody in this class wonders why Septimus commits suicide because "nobody needs PTSD explained." In each of these poems literature is a bridge to realities in the poet's life and the lives of her students.

The synaptic crossings that are Barker's signature strategy are alive and active in the forty-six pages of "New Poems" in this collection. What is new about them is an increased responsiveness to events in time present: an election, a shooting, a hurricane, along with meditations horticultural and historical, on chocolate, mahogany, stumps, and dirt—in which it is recommended that "you let your bare feet walk on/some bare ground."

"Why Cages" begins "So we can peer in. So a creature / can't hide." This opening made me smile, but the remainder of the poem is no joke at all. Nor is a poem on Matisse's "Jazz" cutouts that takes us via the poet's paper dolls to Ravensbrück surgeons' horrible experiments on prisoners. But then along comes a poem brooding on maternal guilt, healed by Edith Piaf regretting nothing. Barker feels "awe" that Piaf, raised in a brothel, can clear away her gloom "the way currents of rain end a drought, the way / milk lets down from a breast."

Reading Barker it is tempting to forget that pleasure is almost nonexistent in the various schools of today's poetry. One might almost think it taboo, so strictly is the rule of coolness enforced by the poetry police of workshop and journal. In truth, Barker harks back to Keats, perhaps by way of Dylan Thomas and Gerard Manley Hopkins and Theodore Roethke. Fortunately for us, she did not die young; she simply kept maturing, without losing the capacity to be in love. She seems to know exactly how to be in love—with tree stumps sending out sprouts and roots "alive, connected, signaling each other," with Monet and Matisse, with family silver, with solid objects of every sort, with glitter and rot, with other people, from students just beginning to ancestors dying and lovers kissing, with the shimmer of language, and with the profound pleasure and suffering we can find in this world. She is a storyteller of buoyancy and humor, and her poems are like inherited treasures you want to look at, handle, take with you move after move, through your scattered life.

—Alicia Ostriker

NEW POEMS

In the Gallery

All the faces on the canvases, and all
    the moving fleshy faces facing the ones flat and framed
on the walls, the living faces shifting
    to a glimpse of a hooked nose, wrinkled chin, or one black
eye with a drift of braided hair covering
    a cheek, and others full-faced, but never for long, as these
gallery-goers move about, facing one
    frame and then another, as I sift among them, just another
face, and then, suddenly, before me:
    the largest canvas in this wide room, one of Monet's early
Nymphéas, the water lilies' petals seeming
    to shift among rounded leaves, their stems submerged in
layers of murky water, almost as if
    moving the way we are, the way faces from the past sift
into my dreams at night, of some
    people I'd rather forget, and of people whose loss I grieve,
like the woman I sat beside in this same
    museum five years ago, the two of us never shifting while
speaking of our long dead mothers,
    and now, that woman, decades younger than I, has died
too, and how her face drifts to me
    late in the night, and now, right in front of my own face,
a portrait of a man who looks so like
    a man who once held me, his face engraved in the frames
of my mind, his brown eyes sifting
    through this space of so many gallery-goers drifting in this
white room, the way water lilies, their
    colors, shift across a pond's surface, before they go under.

On Salt

Neruda says the salt sings. But how about
      Lot's wife, turned into salt for looking back? I can't
            imagine she was singing. Maybe she turned her own
self into salt, so she'd never forget
      the kitchen where she simmered lentil stew,
            the bed where she suckled her babies. We always
look back at what we've left. The past
      won't stay put. I can never forget my son as
            a toddler, his little chuckle. And I'm still grieving
the loss of my friend whose cancer
      invaded her intestines, liver, kidneys, and finally,
            her pulsing brain. Could salt from tears harden to
a stone pillar? And I wish I could erase
      moments when I've been bullied, flattened
            by comments that sliced through my skin. At times
those tauntings attack me in dreams,
      like salt stinging a wound. Before refrigeration,
            salt kept fish and pork flesh from decay, preserved
our food. Easy to know when to dump
      rotten meat, that stink. But not so easy to know
            when or how to dump a memory. How we work
to hold onto silvery moments, take selfies,
      post on Facebook, print photos and slip them
            into leather-covered albums. And the way we hate
forgetting, losing names, dates. How we
      fear Alzheimer's, the brain's wiring gone
            awry. But if we remember too much, we might be
paralyzed, turned into a salty rock-hard
      column. Is that what happened to Lot's wife? It's
            a metabolic process: our brain's designed to forget
most details. That's how it forms impressions,
      makes good judgments. The case in the 1920s of

      "S," who remembered every single detail of his life,
though he understood nothing. And now,
        suddenly, I'm remembering: later in his poem,
           Neruda says the salt plain near Antofagasta is singing
of grief. That entire plain, I've read, is ringed
        by mountains and volcanos, cone-shaped, composed
           of hardened lava and ash, some of them active, alive.

One Week after the Election

—*November 2016*

I'm in the ER with my husband,
      a kidney stone, it turns out, stuck up there,
no seed from which anything
      but pain can grow. Stone sober, they say,
and is he ever, grimacing between
      a rock and a hard place. Too bad he doesn't
drink—a little bourbon might
      help. For days I've been rereading Yeats,
"Easter 1916": "All changed,
      changed utterly." Stony, rocky. But no rock
to lean on. The doc now says
      my husband's kidney stone might be too big
for him to pass. "The stone's in
      the midst of all," says Yeats. Nectarine,
apricot pits: seeds like stones,
      swallow one of those, you're in trouble. But
planted in good dirt, seeds can
      press down furry white roots, send out pale
green stems, leaves, then flower,
      fruit again. Sweet flesh surrounding the seed,
the pit. I need to focus more on
      fruit, stop keening over this election. Can't
let it harden me to stone. How
      I wish I could inject some kind of power-
packed seed into my husband's kidney
      stone, let it sprout roots, stems that would
unfurl, splinter his stone into
      minuscule motes to drop out of his sweet
body, join the pebbles and stones
      we'll step on as we walk to the car for me to
drive him home, where we'll munch
      on peaches, biting gingerly to avoid the pit.

About Chocolate

Hurricane Irma is hurtling into the Carribean
    and on into Florida, as India, Nepal, and Bangladesh sink
under water with 1,200 already dead. Meanwhile,
    our friends in southeast Texas are mopping up in the wake
of Hurricane Harvey, so why am I reading
    about a new kind of chocolate, red chocolate, as if dark,
milk, and white chocolate weren't enough. Ruby
    chocolate we've got now, but all these come from the same
cacao plant the Olmec people used even before
    the Mayans. I grew up on it. Hershey bars, Snickers, and
brownies, in my lunch box, after school, and
    after supper. Cocoa before bed. Chocolate, like touch,
releases oxytocin, the "love hormone" that reduces
    stress. Easter Sundays my sisters and I would hunt down
chocolate eggs, peeking behind bookcases and
    the TV. Candy bunnies, fluffy chicks. And all the chocolate,
oxytocin. But how much could a carton of Mars Bars
    help folks floating in their front yards? And truckloads of
Baby Ruths couldn't rescue little kids harvesting
    cocoa beans in West Africa who, I've now learned, are
routinely—even with "Fair Trade"—kidnapped,
    handed machetes to cut bean pods from the trees, often
slicing their own flesh. They couldn't have
    seen the ads for chocolate: "Comfort in every bar." "Get
the sensation." I just finished Sacha Batthyány's
    memoir. In 1945, during a party with Gestapo bosses
in a castle near the old Austro-Hungarian border,
    at the nearby train depot two hundred Jews were digging
a pit. After dinner, the guests were handed
    guns. Some drove, some walked to the station. They filled
the pit. There had been wine, followed by

cognac, with chocolate. Now I'm remembering the time
when my sisters and I were visiting our
      grandparents, they served us a chocolate-cream pie that—
we found—swarmed with black ants.

The Dirt

A neighbor across the street has paved over his
          whole front yard. Easier to hose off the dog shit,
he says. No dirt in the house, no need to scrape
          his feet at the door. But dirt isn't only filth, nasty
stuff. It's the soil our spinach and potatoes
          grow from. In the Bible, the first human's name:
Adam, meaning earth. And the latest "dirt" on
          dirt—we're running out. That's the skinny, our
dirt's grown skinny. From the Koran: "They
          tilled the soil and populated it in greater numbers
to their own destruction." All this year our own
          neighborhood's been surrounded by earth movers,
clanking, beeping machines: wheel loaders, dump
          trucks, bulldozers, back and forth over acres of
former woods, native grasses, the live oaks
          and juniper already chain-sawed down and hauled
off. Flattening the ground to make way for
          another pharmacy, another body spa, nail salon,
more storage units. Scrape it up. Skin of the earth,
          soil. The interface between rocks and plants and
animals, including us. The poet Roethke: "God
          bless the ground, I shall walk softly there." I guess
my neighbor's never read Roethke, would think
          his poems just "horse pucky," not realizing how
animal feces nourish the earth. In 1916,
          Vladimir Simkhovitch argued that lack of dirt
caused the decline of the Roman Empire. Even
          Lucius Junius Moderatus Columella, writing in
AD 60, noted that Rome's agricultural
          problems were due to farmers' poor treatment

of the soil. I remember the mud pies we made
       as children, feet sloshing in sloppy dirt. And our
parents smiled. Shall I tell the neighbor
       about the new process called "earthing"? Simple
enough, you let your bare feet walk on
       some bare ground. I need to do this. Dirt, we've
now learned, contains antidepressant
       microbes that cause serotonin levels to rise, is
better than Prozac, and with no side effects.

That Bell for Ethel

Small brass dome under the edge of the round
  mahogany table, or oval, with leaves if they
    had company. Like us, for instance, in seersucker
  shorts and blouses, flown in on Grandpop's
nickel from our cramped Tucson tract house
  and scratchy bermuda grass to this upscale
    Jersey suburb, with acres of manicured lawns
  between neighbors, with beds of blossoming
dahlias, roses. That bell, upside-down dome
  with its black nipple of a button for Grandma
    to press when she wanted Ethel to bring more
  biscuits or Parker House rolls, more buttered
corn on the cob, more mashed potatoes—
  or to tell Ethel we were ready for the lemon
    meringue pie. That bell with its cord attached on
  the table's shadowy underside running down
one carved leg, then under the "Oriental"
  rug leading through the pantry and into
    the kitchen, where Ethel spent hours preparing
  menus miraculous to me, so used to my
mother's TV dinners, hamburgers, Bird's
  Eye frozen peas, macaroni and cheese. But
    oh, Ethel's kitchen! With its polished Revere Ware
  and lead-heavy cast-iron skillets, a cupboard
smelling of ginger and cinnamon. After
  lunch, dinner, dishes cleared, the china and
    silver washed and dried, the kitchen scrubbed,
  she climbed the back stairs—barely wider
than her starched-white-uniformed body
  and lit with a single hanging bulb—to
    a 7' x 9' room under the attic. They allowed her

one weekend a month to take the train
into the Bronx to see her sisters
        and sons, people I never met, never
                learned anything about. But I wish I did know
        who they were, could find them, tell
them how I hated the way the grown-ups,
        over their ice-chilled highballs, made fun
                of Ethel, how they guffawed at her notion that
        crops would thrive if planted in sync with
cycles of the moon. Ethel, who
        responded to the dinging of that little
                brass bell in a half-minute, was "colored," and we,
        of course, were not. Today that bell
dangles from a fragment of cord
        under the table that's mine now, the table
                I sort and fold laundry on, a job Ethel did for
        Grandma (who couldn't open a can of
Campbell's soup). Decades since
        that bell's been disconnected, though
                its sharp edges now hang down so far below
        the table's lip that if we sit right under it
and lift a leg too quickly, our jeans
                or skirt will be sliced through to white skin.

After the Shooting in Tucson

—January 2011

Minute by minute how we stared from our cushioned room
at the breaking news, crowd gunned down

outside a Safeway. Catalinas' brown-purple crags a backdrop
for the TV's gloom about the bullet shot

through a congresswoman's skull. Over and over her name,
Gabrielle Giffords. And then, that night, as

President Obama's voice urged us to act with good will,
quoting from Arnold's "Dover Beach,"

I quivered with the electric rush I'd felt as a girl when Daddy
read Keats to us after dinner, his tattered

high-school anthology in one hand, a long-ashed cigarette
in the other. The sight of those mountains,

the sound of a poem out loud, and I was thrown back
to the first year I taught, not far from

the Catalinas, when Sally, Lizbeth, and Gwen lingered
after school and we'd read Eliot together,

puzzling over his "muttering retreats," wondering about
that "overwhelming question." But little

did we know as we sounded those luscious syllables,
on the Salt River Pima-Maricopa Reservation

barely a mile away, kids younger than our little sisters were
pulled from their homes and crowded

into dorms at the Indian School in Phoenix where matrons
shaved their heads and showered them

in kerosene, stripped away their names, dressed them in
new ones like "Bobby" and "Susan." Where

songs of the saguaro, the dove, names of grandmothers,
mountains, the river were erased. Replaced

with electric clock alarms. Before he died, I asked
to record my father's voice, his voice

I couldn't bear to lose. "Fled is that music . . . Do I wake

or sleep?" he'd murmur, as I sat upright
            in my chair, as I did when Obama recited, "Ah love,
let us be true / To one another!" To think
            that, all along, I'd believed we were learning how.

On Stain Removal

My old washer's rubber gasket catches
     the new sheets in its maw, black goop
staining the white, the beige, and even
     when I bleach them, dark traces remain,
the way I've never cleaned out my old
     guilt, bone-aching pain from the time
I said spiteful things about my dying
     mother in the hospital bed, thinking
if she couldn't talk, she couldn't hear,
     a notion corrected by the nurse who
came in and whispered to my mother,
     mentioning to me and my sisters how
hearing is the last of the senses to go,
     or from the way I once read a poem
making fun of my ten-year-old son
     when he was trapped in the audience
and I don't blame him if he's never
     forgiven me. I know even dry cleaners
won't get the stains out of my new
     sheets, and other than these dark gashes,
they're still functional, like me, with
     age spots, snaking veins, and distended
joints defacing my hands as I'm
     once again making the bed, trying to
straighten, smooth these sheets
     under the weight of mended blankets.

Sour Take

Folks sure do love their sugar. Especially
      godly church folk, their pot lucks with all
          those desserts, cookies, cakes and pies
and everyone saying, "Oh I really
      shouldn't," then helping themselves
          to more. All the while chirping and
cooing to each other. Oh, how we
      crave peachy sweet lives, have another
          slice. "Sugar in the morning, / Sugar in
the evening, / Sugar at Suppertime," sang
      the McGuire Sisters in 1958, as I was
          growing up on popsicles, ice cream,
chocolate chip cookies. Years later, I'd
      overload my Visa card following
          Julia Child's recipes in *Mastering the Art
of French Cooking*: Charlotte Malakoff, Soufflé
      Rothschild. What was dinner for friends
          without a heavenly dessert? But no sugar
for me any more—my blood sugar levels
      soar, only to plummet, not into a fiery,
          but a limp, paralyzed hell. In a restaurant,
everyone begging me to order
      the chocolate cream pie, the cheesecake,
          and they don't get it when I say I really,
really don't want even a single
      slippery bite. Sugar highs, sugar
          lows. Reminds me of the low-down on
the history of sugar, sugar cane,
      a tropical grass discovered in India

by the Persians between the 6th and 4th
centuries BC. Columbus first brought
          sugar to the Caribbean, where slaves
                    were shipped and forced to hook their
backs over the fields. And in our own
          country's Southern colonies: slaves
                    fed the sweet tooth of good white
folks, who loved their Red Velvet
          Cake, their Ultimate Hummingbird
                    Cake, their Coconut Cake. Sweets
for the sweet. And those plantation
          owners fed their slaves sugar, one way
                    to keep them going. Eight times
more addictive than cocaine, sugar. And
          what about candies folks love to suck on
                    today? Milk Duds, Malted Milk Balls,
and Sugar Babies: all coated with a glaze
          made from beetle shit. And what's that
                    turbulent smoke in Brazil looking like
a nuclear bomb's been detonated? Every
          May through November, sugar cane
                    fields are set aflame to burn green and dry
leaves off the stalks so harvesting takes
          less labor, owners get more bang for
                    their buck. Air so bad people's lungs
clog. Of course, I've got to admit,
          when my friend calls me "Sugar," and
                    my man calls me his very own "Sweetie,"
I lap it up. "Be my little sugar, /And

love me / All the time," sang that famous
            trio of sisters. But since my body runs with
the metabolism of a hummingbird, I burn
            calories like crazy, need fatty red meat
                        to keep from descending into sourness and
worse. Come to think of it, I'd rather
            be somebody's fat—or solid protein—
                        neither heavenly nor hellish, but sticking
to the ribs, with staying power for
            a good long time. Yet I can't forget how
                        cattle are rounded up, prodded onto trucks,
run through chutes to have their
            throats cut, their bodies hung from
                        steel hooks and carved into pieces to fit
between shrink wrap and styrofoam.

Why Cages

So we can peer in. So a creature
        can't hide. Zoos keep jaguars in 9-gauge
chain-link pens. Wild, these cats
        race across grasslands faster than a bicyclist
with the Tour de France. Parrots
        fly a hundred miles a day, but caged,
they'll bite their feet, bellies, till
        they bleed. "Zoochosis": psychosis caused
by confinement. Our ancestors
        lived in caves, but that's not the same as
being locked up. "Give me land,
        lots of land, under starry skies above, don't
fence me in," crooned Bing Crosby
        in 1943. How much open space do we
humans need? A student of mine
        signed up with a college group volunteering
to be jailed for a week. She said
        before long, they all began sobbing, raging,
and none of them was even
        confined in solitary. I've never stepped inside
a prison. But I've been kept
        alone in a medical ward, electrodes taped
across my body, one small
        window for interns to peer in at me, a loud-
speaker over my head, a voice
        booming in at random moments. I seldom
scream, but I did, again and again.

On Scissors and Matisse

In old age he used scissors to create
           Jazz, the cutouts everyone raves about, those
    primal colors. All done by a man
           in a wheelchair, post-colostomy. Can't they see
how in those red, green, yellow
           shapes, hearts fan into flames, stars shatter
    into grenades? His "Sword Swallower":
           no exuberant circus performer, no songster
with notes springing from his mouth,
           but a head wrenched back, jaws forced open
    as swords pierce his throat, knives
           slicing a tongue. At three, my tonsillectomy:
a phony promise of ice cream before
           waking in a ward with a hundred children
    lined up in cots, parents forbidden
           for a week, no touching permitted, screams
at night, constant sounds of gurneys
           rattling, glare of the yellow-lighted doors
    into surgery. What kinds of blades were
           used for tonsillectomies? I think of my prized
 nickel-plated scissors that cut
           through white space around the figures
    in my paper doll books. 1940s, with
           WWII exploding, the bedridden Matisse
learned his daughter had been
           tortured by the Gestapo, forced onto a cattle
    train to Ravensbrück. Not much
           older than three when I saw *Life*'s photos
of Buchenwald's survivors. Bodies

shrunk to papery skin stretched over
jutting bones. What fractures splayed
                    behind those eyes? Impossible to see inside
the paper dolls' figures, their pink-toned
                    flesh. Matisse's daughter Marguerite jumped
          from the train before it reached
                    Ravensbrück, hid out in the Vosges Mountains'
pine forests till fellow resisters
                    rescued her. I'd take care with my scissors
          never to slice a paper doll's
                    arm or hip. How old do you need to be
before you discern the forms
                    under the forms of Matisse's cut outs? Before
          you learn of the friend who watched
                    from her bedroom window as her brother
set himself on fire, of the sister
                    who saw a man drop from twenty stories,
          a lake of blood five feet from
                    her Capezio flats, and of the friend hauled
by a crazed 'Nam vet into his bedroom
                    and raped in the ass for two hours, his loaded
          .45 beside her head. Before you learn
                    the muscles, bones, nerves of Ravensbrück's
inmates were cut out, implanted in
                    other prisoners' bodies, the incisions injected
          with bacteria, wood shavings, ground
                    glass. How to speak of a tonsillectomy? After,
my mother said, I was never the same.

In My Seventy-Sixth Year

We need a new roof. No gale force wind has
                ripped it off, it's a matter of age. The skin
      of our house has thinned,
like mine. No crisis, no dearth of power or clean
                water as in Puerto Rico after Hurricane Maria,
      no walls blackened or splintered
like those from California's wildfires. At least
                newscasters label these "catastrophes," not
      "issues," a word everyone
uses now for a neighbor's fuss over fence lines
                or a three-million-gallon oil spill. We don't
      need anything fancy, no
dome or mansard, no gambrel or skillion, I just
                need a well-braced shield to keep me from
      lung-flattening news, from
the fact that our poor world reels and not from
                issues but from calamities, and from the way
      my own past blunders
leak through my ceiling like the rancid blather
                of some politicians. I'm grappling with how
      old age can make us
porous, unable to pull into the hard-muscled shell
                of a younger, stronger self. These fissures in
      my roof let thoughts of my
dead seep through, what I said, or didn't say,
                and wish I had. Portuguese have the word
      saudade, a longing for what
once had been, for those no more alive and
                chattering beside us. Roof above the head:
      shelter, insulation, a basic

need. But no tightly seamed roof, thick-shingled
             with sword-sharp edges, can fend off all
        the squalls, the hitches,
crises, issues that might be swirling nearby,
             can guard the tissue-thin skin of my walls.

In Praise of Stumps

Dumb as a stump, they say. My neighbor
   hates stumps, and, after sawing down half
the trees on his manicured acre, wants all
   the stumps removed. Eyesores, they take
up space on his lawn. Not an easy job,
   stump removal. Grinders cost at least
a hundred bucks a day to rent, and he'd
   need goggles, a chain saw, a pick mattock,
digging bar, and a shovel. Potassium nitrate
   works, with a drill and kerosene. Years ago,
I'd planned to rid my yard of its scraggly
   stumps, till I learned the roots of trees feed
each other, pump sugar into a stump
   to keep it from dying and the stump will
send out new sprouts that can lift into
   saplings, and then, in time, into full-sized
trees. I hadn't known that stumps offer
   nesting sites for chickadees, titmice, owls,
and woodpeckers, shelter for chipmunks,
   shrews, salamanders, and foxes. But my
neighbor's not the only one in this
   suburban enclave with codes more rigid
than a concrete slab: grass over six inches
   high bordering the street and you're in
for a big fine. I'm thinking of Hopkins'
   "Long live the weeds." I like our grasses
tall enough to ripple in the wind,
   so native salvias can bloom and feed
the butterflies and hummingbirds. Sick
   of tidiness, the desire to emulate British
country estates with our faux scaled-

down mini-mansions floating on green
carpet no one ever touches, other than
        a hired man on his ride-'em mower who
keeps the outdoors outside, keeps anyone
        from taking too deep a breath, from any
Whitmanesque desire to go live with
        the animals, which I'm fantasizing I might
want to do, but right now, I'll go out,
        speak to my dead trees, tell them I know
their roots are alive, connected to all
        the leafy trees nearby, and I know they're
signaling each other through an
        arboreal internet, their intricate fungal,
mycelial network, maybe warning
        about our thick, dumb-as-a-ditch skulls.

Rilke to Roethke on Rosh Hashanah

"Lord it is time"—past time—for
        our country's political bombast and vitriol
to end, for the South Texas heat
        to drop, for my crammed Inbox to clear,
for relief from knowing my old friend
        who's not even old has only a few weeks left
on this over-warmed planet with oceans
        so littered with plastic bags, bottles, duct tape,
balloons, six-pack rings, drinking straws,
        and rubber duckies that dolphins and whales
choke, suffocate, and end up beached
        on our coasts, but it's Rosh Hashanah, Jewish
New Year, time for reflection, renewal,
        time for believing earth will go on—so maybe
when the oaks, mesquite, hackberries bare
        their branches, while, as Rilke says, the "dry
leaves are blowing," there'll be room to see
        stars as well as the branches, stems, nodes that
birthed the leaves, to study the furrows
        of the cedar elms' underpinnings, so I turn from
Rilke to Roethke, to the "urge, wrestle,
        resurrection of dry sticks," that "sucking and
sobbing" of "cut stems struggling
        to put down feet," and then, finally, I remember:
"In a dark time the eye begins to see,"
        and I know, if this is Roethke's "purity of pure
despair," it's time, past time—on this
        day that resounds with a ram's horn—I struggle
to lie down, rest, grow from the dark.

On Delta Flight #2164 from JFK

I'm headed home from a stint at Long Island's
Walt Whitman Birthplace, a day after
      visiting Dickinson's Amherst Homestead. With
her thread-laced fascicles, Emily liked
      to see a train "lap the miles," but at jet speed,
we're hardly lapping. Along with Walt,
      I find crowds "curious," and, as an introvert
with an extrovert bent, I always want to
      know everyone's stories, since we're all part of
the "eternal float of solution." But right
      now I'm jammed in a middle seat among 524
passengers, and the silent man on my left
      drapes his hairy fingers over the armrest. His
thick head blocks the window. I'm hardly
      floating. Whenever I'm in a plane, part of me
is stuck in 1947, not yet five, waving
      to my sobbing grandma at La Guardia before
flying with my straight-backed mother
      and toddling sister across the United States all
the way to Phoenix. Clouds rippled
      beyond the window, billowing threads. But then
I didn't see my East Coast grandma
      for four years. The way she'd held me in her lap
while dropping stitches from her
      rumpled knitting. Who was I without her blue
eyes meeting mine? Even now, whenever I
      leave home, I fear I won't return, will lose touch,
become "Nobody." Maybe that's why I'm
      always bantering with strangers in our tangled

strands as we board and deplane. If they're

    chatting with me, I could be somebody. Yet I

must keep my own skin intact, and though

    I wish, like Walt, I could be "loos'd of limits and

imaginary lines," I must hold to a few

    limits or I'd lose my whole self. "The Soul selects

her own Society," says Dickinson, but

    who am I in this crowd? Always, as Emily laments,

"the bewildering thread." I need to fasten

    my own threads the way warp strands on a wooden

loom are tightened, so the weave will hold.

Not Montale's Eel

These fluttering creatures brushing
　　　　our windshields, littering our highways and lawns:
snout-nosed butterflies on the move
　　　　this fall for a solid month, drawn by the dangling
fruit of hackberries, trees tidy folk
　　　　call "trash," but with perfect fuel for these twenty
million headed to the Rio Grande—
　　　　and somehow I start thinking of Montale's eel,
la sirena infiltrating *gorielli di melma*,
　　　　　vast "pockets of mud," though I'm embarrassed
to remember how, when first translating
　　　　the poem, I assumed the eel was male, like a lone
sperm making his determined journey
　　　　upstream only to die unless he'd beaten all the other
guys to the ovum, and of course
　　　　I can't forget Monty Python's hilarious "Every
Sperm is Sacred," so then I wonder about
　　　　the millions of migrations from the first time
a single cell from the ocean drifted
　　　　to land, beginning a series of transformations
leading to our own species that's spread
　　　　itself across the globe, often, like butterflies,
struggling to find food, or sometimes
　　　　to wipe out neighbors and lay claim to silver, oil,
or fertile loam, and of course, thousands
　　　　of these butterflies are devoured by the chickadees
and titmice that normally empty our
　　　　backyard bird feeders, though I guess it's always
about moving from one place to another,
　　　　each of us food for someone else, or there wouldn't
be life at all, and I know we don't want

existence to be a stagnant pool with no whirligig
beetles or dragonflies, but I sure don't
    feel like "sister" to that gleaming eel of Montale's—
some days I'd like to stay put on solid
    clay that will hold my feet steady, but I guess it's all
a matter of motion, the release
    of CO_2 so oxygen can travel through capillaries;
migrations, even the poet's
    l'iride breve, "brief iris," won't flower without roots,
tentacles swimming through dirt.

In the Galápagos

Though Melville called these islands
           a pile of "Cinders dumped here and there"
                      with "a wailing spirit," I don't want ashes
of his morbid mental state to smother
           my memory of bobbing in a fiberglass
                      panga where at first I saw only the *garua*,
the stratocumulus hovering over tips
           of volcanoes, mist that drapes the rocks
                      in a whitened haze, so I wasn't even sure
we'd reached a place that's real. It all
           shifted, the way for an instant we'd
                      see a whale's flukes, a tail flashing above
the ocean, and gone. Then, straight
           ahead, splatters of bird droppings
                      like paint streaks on stone, but the paint
moved, the rocks teeming with
           white-feathered, blue-footed boobies,
                      their beaks and outsize feet a brighter
blue than any sky I've ever seen
           as we anchored off Isla Fernandina
                      and hiked a hummocky field of ropy
pahoehoe lava, when I almost tripped
           on a rock-black tail, no, hundreds upon
                      hundreds of iguanas warming like soft-
bellied dollops of stone, the only
           sound besides our whispering the hiss
                      of brine spewed through their nostrils,
salt-caked, white as the guano
           under them. And beyond, palo santo
                      trees, holy sticks so laced with lichen

their whiteness shimmered at noon
        as if by moonlight. Not Melville's end
                of the world, but a beginning, air so fresh
I felt I'd grown new lungs. When
        I walked on Isla Isabela's sand alongside
                a great blue heron, and sat down to rest
in the midst of a dozen nursing
        sea lions, I didn't spot any of the creatures
                our kind have carried with us, the rats
pigs, dogs, cats that eat the eggs
        of the giant tortoises. I remember
                that, while exploring Chatham Island,
Darwin noted he'd met an "immense
        Turpin" and was mesmerized. But
                did he know, in the years surrounding
his voyage, crews like his—and
        Melville's—hauled off thousands
                of those tortoises, stacked them flipped
on their backs in the ship's hold,
        where they survived for months
                without food? I keep thinking of the flightless
cormorant—steady on her nest
        of marine grass and algae over
                rock, on an island where nothing has
ever been mined, hammered, or
        soldered, where the lava hasn't
                been crumbled to pebbles—who sits
within a circle of her own
        shit, above a cloud-gray chick
                and one still whole, unbroken egg.

After Reading Baudelaire

With sky a tight-fitting cast-iron lid,
       humidity and temp ninety-eight, rain stalled
over the next county, I listen to Edith
       Piaf, her raunchy, chutzpah-laden contralto—
je ne regrette rien, she growls and purrs,
       as if she actually believes she has no regrets,
although I sure do, have never eased
       the ache of leaving my baby boy with sitters
so I could keep on with grad school,
       how some nights I'd come home to a bundle
of shuddering sobs till I held him
       and nursed him, but now of course, he's grown,
a solid forty-one, and I'm proud as
       any proud mom can be, yet I can't shake free
of those tangling webs, while I know
       the spleen isn't what Baudelaire and his cronies
thought, rather a neighbor of the stomach
       churning out antibodies, blasting worn-out red
blood cells, not the seat of down-in-
       the-mouthness and foul temper as medieval
physiologists believed, so maybe I'm just
       cleaning away forty-plus years of regret, because
I'd sure like to sing along with Piaf
       that I regret nothing, and, after all, I wasn't as
bad as other mothers I've read about,
       even Martha Sharp, who during the SS Nazi
years left her own offspring for months
       at a time to rescue Jewish kids and bring them
to the U.S., saving them from Auschwitz
       and Treblinka, saintly to be sure, but I wouldn't
blame her children for feeling some

      pretty sour spleen about a mom's not being
there to hug them for winning archery
      medals at summer camp or battling measles
or bronchitis, so I hunker down again
      with Piaf—her *laissez-vous faire, Milord*—in awe
that, decades after a girlhood in
      her grandmother's brothel, this "Little Sparrow"
is even now clearing my gloom,
      the way currents of rain end a drought, the way
milk lets down from a breast.

In Light of the Eclipse

Three celestial bodies it takes, the sun,
        moon, and our earth. And now, in a single day:
                visits by two old friends who propel me back to selves
I inhabited decades ago, and by my grown
        son, who's returning portraits of ancestors he hasn't
                room for. How these gilt-framed nineteenth-century
pastels spiral me down to the year
        I turned five when my parents moved us away
                from my silky-skinned Grandma, East Coast red oaks
and flowering dogwoods to the prickly
        Phoenix dustbowl of the forties. We're not even
                in the direct path of the eclipse, but all these orbitings
from years back shift the way I see
        my own face in the mirror, and what I see is
                not what I'm used to seeing. A red-tailed hawk has
swirled around the house and lands
        on a branch inches from my window, hunches
                there all afternoon. Not a glimpse of the finches,
wrens, cardinals that always flutter
        around our yard. The room is breathing an odd
                shadow. But the moon only appears to cover the fire
that gives our planet life. The orbits that
        govern us, circles within circles, one sphere
                moving into another. Now in this uncanny light,
I find a bird's nest cradled on a sumac
        limb, a woven round of leaves and twigs,
                and I wonder if it's waiting to be filled. Or if a clutch
of eggs has hatched and nestlings have
        flown—or if the dark circle in its center
                means it's been abandoned. The word "eclipse": from
the Greek "to vanish." Yet today I'm

recovering vision all these years have clouded
over. How the bustle of a sunlit life can eclipse earlier
selves within us. Is the moon
over the sun's orb a closing? Or an opening.

Lifted

Cardinals, finches, chickadees flock
      to our feeders. Up to four thousand feathers
on each bird's little body. On a tundra
      swan: twenty-five thousand. "Light as a feather,"
we like to say, as opposed to "this
      too too solid flesh," or my stiff and creaking
joints. But even dry feathers aren't
      so light. Headdresses Las Vegas show girls
wear will hold two thousand plumes,
      weigh twenty pounds. All the rage, feathers,
especially for hats in the late nineteenth
      century. Women's toques were even topped
with stuffed whole birds. In 1886,
      on the streets of New York, Frank Chapman
counted over forty species of feathers
      on bonnets, caps, cloches, down brims. I guess
we earthbound humans have always
      yearned to fly. I'm no Icarus, but oh, how I wish
I could transform my flabby arms
      into wings. Last June as I stepped onto a Gulf
Coast pier, I stopped. Two yards
      down on the wooden slats stood a great blue
heron. We stared at each other for,
      I swear, ten minutes, before he opened wide his
long wings and, shrieking, flew off to
      a hill beyond, a sight staying with me wherever
I drop my feet. Sometimes when I'm
      happy, I'll flap my arms. Just feeling that motion
makes me smile. During Brahms's Fourth
      Symphony last night, as I leaned my aching back
against the concert hall's padded seat,
      the violinists' bows rose like feathery quills, and
a thousand listeners sprouted wings.

Circlings

—*In memoriam, Jeannine Keenan*

∞

Pacing across the bamboo floor,
            I stop inside each sunlit circle cast
by seven skylights in my roof,
            marveling that all day these disks drift
across the room, and how
            she would have loved to know of my
little ritual, but I can't tell her,
            she's been gone for months, and for
months before, she couldn't even
            step from her bedroom by herself,
her sentences so garbled I had to
            guess at what she was laboring to say,
but I wish I could tell her
            about the way light travels through
the day, and how I try to step
            within each single round as if I could
hold onto the light, as if she
            could fit within one of these spheres.

∞

Sections of a grapefruit sliced
            in half, fibrous rays fanned from its core,
a yellow glimmer she would
            have relished, and now, six garlic cloves
around their stem, spokes of
            a wheel, plump white bulbs nestled into
the center; and I see that an
            apple core, sliced crossways, resembles

a rose window like one she—

        as a child—would have knelt beneath.

∞

In the parking lot of our
        neighborhood grocery store, a grackle,
with its round eye, catches
        mine till it lifts above the cracked asphalt,
and I think of Stevens, whose
        lines she'd often quote, with his blackbird
flying beyond sight, marking
        "the edge / Of one of many circles."

∞

The shock—the way she went,
        together with her husband of sixty years,
the pair encircling their sagging
        bed with photos of daughters, grandkids,
favorite books and the tigers and
        lions she'd sewn, stuffed, plush creatures
she'd brought almost to life from
        chenille and thread, and then—he gave
her the pills, and only after he
        knew she'd left, sent one shot to his head,
leaving only a small circle of blood
        on the pillow, but not before he'd called
911 to report what he'd done
        and was about to do, and then—the news:

even on TV, and the phone
        calls among those of us who loved her, circling.

∞

The star jasmine vine outside
        our front door, a spiralling around
the porch, filaments clinging
        to an upright post, and I'm swung
back to years when her sturdy
        arms cradled a new gift, a woolen
shawl, a wooden bowl, a basket
        she wove from reeds of a pond she
once loved but left, and
        now her leaving tangles the coils
of my body's core, till I'm
        left leaning on any post I can find.

∞

I try to peel an apple so the skin
        remains in one unbroken spiral,
but it breaks in pieces, as my blunt
        knife, that she would have known
how to sharpen, slips from its path.

∞

Under the lines of the cross,
        beneath a horizontal slash through
a vertical stripe, far below
        the towers of those medieval cathedrals

she'd visited so often,
                  the labyrinth, spiraled path mirroring
the old circles of our long
                  journeys, seeming repetitions, endlessness
 of our steps, and yet, how
                  we keep on, one foot, the other, not
wandering, but a gradual
                  swirl to the center, small place to rest.

                  ∞

Always sunflowers she wanted,
                  for birthdays, any occasion, even saying
that, if somehow she could
                  return after she'd died, she'd be a sunflower—so
after she left, we scattered
                  sunflower seeds over her ashes, and now,
by the roadsides on our drive
                  to the coast: acres and acres of seed-packed
heads swiveling throughout
                  the day, each round with its seeds following
Fibonacci's sequence, which
                  she knew, as she knew of Yeats' gyres,
the way things turn, return,
                  a phenomenon—I'd almost forgotten—
she labeled "the spiral surprise."

from **GLOSS** (2020)

What Surfaces

Another chip in the white enameled sink, only three years old. How
                I've tried to keep it pristine, and yet—
      stainless steel pots scrape it till the black
cast iron breaks through. What's below a surface gloss. Now the flesh
             on my hands has grown so thin
     the layers underneath show through,
rivery veins and knobby metacarpals. Knuckles like pebbles—like
              rocks. I've bordered my rose beds
     with stones from Blanco Creek. How long
did it take to shape those irregular rounds and ovals? Our house, built
            of blocks mined from the quarry only
     five miles up the road—limestone
formed in the Paleozoic Era. My favorite paperweight: a fossilized
            clam I found in the backyard, remains
     from the time the land around us
lived under ocean. Something so pocked, wizened, holding my papers
            in place. Arriving at the Grand Canyon,
     we've all peered down at those
dozens of rock layers—granite, dolomite, sandstone, shale, basalt—
            formed two million, maybe two billion
     years ago. And who would want
to mend that great magenta-, purple-, blood-shaded rip in the earth's
            surface? It's what we come for,
     to gawk at all those layers, exposed.

Silk Roads

Such a quiet act, the needle penetrating cloth. Loops of thread in coral, pink, fuchsia, teal, turquoise, forest green, lime, lemon, mustard, royal purple, brown, and black. The design dotted in crisp dark blue on the linen. A butterfly, a road.

The Great Silk Road. Overland. But by the time my great-grandfather set off mid-nineteenth century to find more silk for Macclesfield's mills in Cheshire, he traveled by sea. The story goes he sailed up the Yangtze to ask the Chinese to trade. But how far upriver and on what sort of boat?

All from a worm, the caterpillar of a moth. Larvae of silverfish, wasps, mayflies, lacewings, and thrips produce silk, too, though not of good quality. Not used for textiles. And not for embroidery. Glossy three-ply filaments satin-stitching, chain-stitching leaves, wings, ridges in a winding path.

The prow of a ship cutting through water, the spray of droplets glistening in the light. A steel needle pricking the gaps between the woven linen threads, the needle emerging from underneath, poked back to the surface.

I don't know what Great-Grandfather offered to trade for silk, only that the Chinese told him to go back where he came from. But overnight a typhoon ripped the current. In the morning, village elders boarded the battered ship, said they'd trade with this white devil, the spirits had willed it.

The pupas are dipped in boiling water or pierced with a needle. Then the cocoon is unraveled as a continous thread. How a boat knifes its way through a current, lifting ripples, a wake. I want to slice through this story, unspool its lengths. Great-Grandfather didn't speak Mandarin. Who translated? Who traveled with him? Did trackers drag the ship through shallows, narrows of the Yangtze's Three Gorges, hauling that weight? And who paid whom for what?

Some embroideries are never finished. And even if we try to keep the underside tidy, to avoid messy knots and threads, it's hard to see a pattern on the back of the cloth, where the colors, even while shimmering, snarl.

"Elegant," She Said

My new friend was chuckling, saying she cracked up when I let fly
the "f" word while speaking to an audience
of five-hundred because, she said, I look so "elegant, a class act,
a knockout." I changed the subject. She doesn't
get it. Growing up, I was always the clumsy one, by sixth grade
inhabiting a close-to-six-foot, rib-protruding,
hunched-over frame, buck teeth in braces, wispy blonde hair, pale
bluish eyes. Called "Scarecrow" and "String Bean" by
other kids. Then in high school, "Boobless Bean." And with
a regal-shouldered, chocolate-eyed, russet-haired
mother who modeled for the fashion pages of *The Tucson Daily
Citizen.* My brunette little sister: "the pretty one":
began Flair Modeling School at fourteen. Clairol's 1950s ads
asked, "Do blondes have more fun?" Not this
blonde. The time I brought my drawing of a girl to show
Daddy and his only comment was a clipped,
"She's not very pretty." Over my parents' Old-Fashioneds,
banter about women: "pert little nose, a shame
about her piano legs"; "good-hearted, but that horrendous
pitted skin." Now the flesh of my arms droops
like crumpled silk. Yet my husband swears he loves my
bones. Once, when Mom was around my age,
she spoke of her granny Lilian Walker Graves, who sparkled on
the vaudeville stage. "Men tripped on their
shoe strings at the sight of her, "Mom said. "And my own
mother," she went on, "had that same quality,
just as I did, and—as your little sister does," she added, looking
at the ceiling. But then, the year before Mom
died in the retirement home, as I walked beside her electric cart
while she steered past wheelchairs, canes, and
walkers, a resident stopped us: "Why Pam," she gushed, "This

daughter of yours—no one would question

you're her mother! She looks just like you, moves with your elegance, your grace." Mom jerked upright and

sputtered, "She *does?*" and pressed her foot on the accelerator, whizzing off. I had to run to catch up with her.

Ivory Carvings

How it swelled in the bathroom sink, Granny's cardboard pellet. A basin full of water, and then, a slow unfurling—petals, a lotus. And more petals, rose, lavender, yellow, abloom in the chipped sink we spat in while brushing our teeth.

The lotus petals signal an expansion of the soul. Or were those paper flowers chrysanthemums? For Confucius, objects of meditation. In China even now, symbols of vitality.

For years on my living-room wall—in intricate high relief, nine inches in diameter—a chrysanthemum made of ivory, poised on its stem, and set on a black background in a two-by-five-foot frame. Once it hung in Granny's high-ceilinged hallway in Hong Kong. Carved from an elephant's tusk.

How these creatures mourn their dead, circle the body, caress it with their trunks. Flap their ears, click their tusks, entwine their trunks when reuniting. Big money for those tusks, long, curved incisors. White gold.

Favorite bedtime reading, in Granny's voice, "O Best Beloved," how the elephant's child got his trunk, a painful stretching of his little nose by a crocodile. No mention of his tusks, although in Kipling's drawing they're right there, both of them, pointing toward a banana tree.

By the tenth century, not an elephant left in North Africa. Now from Kenya to Congo to Cameroon, mass killings daily. In Tanzania, villagers roll poisoned pumpkins into the road for elephants to eat.

Bananas—shaped like small tusks. Granny's collection of bric-a-brac included a banana carved from ivory. So clever, she'd say, the way the artist showed it half peeled, as if ready to eat. The petals of my ivory chrysanthemum—a mandala? Or a mouth forced open, jagged stumps, splinters of teeth?

Interior

Those Phoenix dust storms in the forties: a solid wall, brown mass hurtling toward us, as Mom screamed, "Close the windows, close the windows!" and we raced around the house, turning handles. Even so, after, a layer of dirt blurred the lines of every shelf and counter, every table, every cushion. Every book. The bathroom basin.

Where Granny on her visit helped me brush my teeth. Brisk little strokes around and around, up to the attic, she trilled, then to the nursery, down more stairs to the parlor, the drawing room, and, finally, all the way to the cellar. Rooms I'd never known existed.

What dust can do to the lungs—those fragile, spongy organs filled with alveoli. A struggle to breathe. These tiny spaces, miniature rooms within the duplex of the lungs.

Four rooms: two bedrooms, a kitchen, living room in that house. Smoke thickening the air. My father's five packs a day, my mother's half-dozen cigarettes with drinks before their dinner, when they talked and we were not to. In our cots in our room, strict seven o'clock bedtime for my sisters and me, no talking, no questions.

After Granny's visit, my own little mouth held polished hallways leading to rooms with windows glistening to moist lawns, a robin's-egg-blue sky. No dust. Or smoke. No need to open the rattling, rusted screen door to leave a choking house.

Gathering Bones

Like a book, Mom said about life: you turn the page and go on. The same way she moved in and out of houses. Garage sale after sale. Each year like a chapter torn from a novel's spine and hurled.

But some of us go back, looking for patterns. The way a plot builds, chapter upon chapter, like a pelvis resting on the femur, femur on the patella, on the tibia and fibula.

That film I can't forget: *Aftermath*, story of a Catholic Polish farmer who discovers Jewish tombstones buried under the town's road. He's obsessed with digging them up, five-foot, rounded headstones, one by one. Doesn't know why. He plants them in rows, like corn, in his field. Learns Hebrew, reads the inscriptions, names and names.

During the months before she died, when I begged her to talk about her childhood, my mother changed the subject, demanded more milk in her tea.

Let sleeping dogs lie, the villagers, even the young priest, warned that farmer.

Years ago, Mom told me about a nightmare. She was racing, breathless, through a walled, labyrinthian garden to save herself from a gigantic man. How many houses had it taken to escape? New Jersey, Arizona, house after house, different towns, and finally, in less than a decade, three houses in New Hampshire. Each one repainted.

At the film's end, the farmer learns it was his father who'd led the villagers in a round-up of the local Jews, locking them in the family's cottage, which he set on fire.

The night before the family's ceremonial scattering of Mom's ashes on the lake she'd loved, I slept with the cannister beside me. Sunrise, I carried it down to the dock, opened the lid. I reached in, gathered a small handful, and over my arms and legs spread powdery flakes of crushed bone. I slipped then, into the water that carried them, glittering, in the light.

Once I'd dreamed of myself as a toddler, walking down an unlit hospital hall with closed doors on both sides. I was holding my mother's hand. But no, she was gripping mine.

Latent Image

Before she died, Mom pulled that photo out of the album, tore it to shreds. The one that showed her at seven, naked, posed like a nymph, a statue on the lawn. Grandfather's insisting she strip in front of the servants and sit like that, her legs folded to one side, her head bent in the opposite direction. His little nymph.

Stilled, in that photo, caught by silver particles, the standard black and white photographic process introduced in 1871. A photo's final image: metallic silver embedded in a gelatin coating.

"Stills," we say, stopped action, a single frame of a film. Yet I never knew Mom stilled until she died, her trim body beneath a sheet. Always moving, vacuuming every crumb of dust to be sucked into the guts of the Electrolux, its bag emptied into the garbage and gone. After dinner, Ed Sullivan on TV, her hands working a needle or scissors, her feet joggling, toes wriggling. Daytime, her sewing machine's roar, her fingers zipping the fabric toward the needle, her foot pressing the pedal, full speed. And driving, always over the limit, as if to say "get me out of here."

Silver atoms, freed when silver salts meet the light, form an image that's stable. Once the film's developed, it's bathed in a chemical fixer. Clean water clears the fixer from the print, and the latent image becomes permanent.

The story she told me long after I'd moved away: how, when, at thirteen, she asked her mother what she should do about the black hairs spiralling in her armpits, Granny said, "Father can help you with that," and he did, in the shower, every week, shaving her.

Surgery, a Little History

Stunned by the god's "feathered glory," Yeats wrote
          of Leda, in one of my mother's favorite poems. How many
                    painters have rendered this image, of a woman swooning
with a swan. But the trickery, the deceit of Zeus,
          disguising himself. And now, these doctors of mine,
                    with their downy reassurance. Robotic surgery, they coo,
easy as slipping into and out of a pond. Not gods,
          but white-coated, so feathery-voiced I believe them,
                    sign the forms. Their sleek offices, paintings of lakes,
of cool streams on their walls. Such calming
          waters I lie back, feet propped in the metal stirrups,
                    till the speculum is pressed inside, probing for what lies
underneath: stems of water lilies, small
          fish. Scraping the silt. No "sudden blow," the surgeons
                    promise, "minimally invasive, laparoscopic, tiny incisions,
needle-thin instruments. Nothing to fear,"
          they stress. But photos I've now seen online show
                    massive silvery cones, spiked bills that angle like spears
toward the bull's eye of a belly. "Indifferent"
          beaks that peck around inside, pulling sagging
                    organs upright, shoving them into new places, wrapping
them in mesh like the webs between toes of
          swans. "A month," they say. But it's more like
                    twenty before my body's mine again, works again, though
I'm told I'm a lucky one, patients half
          my age may need a catheter for a year, even two,
                    "post-op," and often, they add, women will need
the surgery redone. We say we're "put under"
          an anesthetic. And now that Mom's been gone
                    ten years, I'm sinking down into murk to remember
the time during eighth grade when she

picked me up, surprising me after school, my gray
        Samsonite packed in the Ford's back seat: "We're going
to the hospital, honey, just a little operation,
     so you won't have those awful cramps anymore." After
        the nurse stripped me and tied me into a blue robe that left
my bottom bare, she told my mother
     to leave. They swooped in then, medical students,
        checking for cancer, they said, and pulled aside the gown,
fingered my breasts. The next morning,
     the nurse wheeled me down the hall for the little
        operation. The doctor and his white-jacketed flock were
waiting, thought the anesthetic had
     kicked in. I was awake all during their hooting,
        their laughing. Spread-eagled in the stirrups, the clamp
inside, the scraping. No Yeatsian
     "white rush." The blood that followed. Mom
        never knew. Shortly before she died, she told me how,
the first year she was married, her doctor
     insisted she come to the office Saturday morning. Got
        her on her back, fiddled with her clitoris, diddled her, his
fingers pulsing inside her, experimenting, to
     make her come. The same ob/gyn who delivered me,
        who believed women should suffer in childbirth, no need
for an anesthetic while he rammed those forceps
     deep inside to haul me out. The body holds these
        incisions. For years. And genetic memory exists: we carry
molecular scars. No eggs from such visitations. Only
     hard-boiled knowledge that you won't get the truth
        from these hook-scissored beaks when what they do is tear,
rip into you, and maybe, maybe you'll recover,
     put on new knowledge with your own power. Flap
        back at them, beat your own wings against them. And snap.

Beyond a Certain Age, I Look for Paris in Paris

I know about le Syndrome de Paris, triggered when a greenhorn's
       rosy-lensed image turns muddy, but I'm no wistful
             Francophile neophyte, so why am I
feeling like my British uncle who'd sniped as I left for my first trip
       to Paris: "Why bother with that filth?" When
             my friends heard I was heading
again for the City of Lights, they said "Paris? *oh! yes!*" in a breathy,
       pre-orgasmic voice, as if they were picturing my
             lounging outside a café on
the Boul'Mich over a café au lait or glass of chilled Sauvignon Blanc
       as prelude to a blissful night with my husband in
             a cramped but oh, so charming
chambre double, forgetting that I can't do caffeine or alcohol, and
       that, as I'd also forgotten, in mid-July the sidewalks,
             the Métro, and the galleries would
be chock-a-block with chattering Brits, Italians, Yanks, Germans,
       and Brazilians, along with—since it's the week
             of the Tour de France—clusters
of steel-bodied cyclists, so we're jostled by tee-shirts emblazoned
       with slogans like "Endurance Conspiracy" and
             "Tourminator." The outing we'd
planned to Giverny is canceled, too much traffic, when for months
       I've been yearning to peer down into the waters that
             spawned Monet's *Nymphéas:*
those rounded walls in l'Orangerie, depths that lead to more depths,
       dissolving boundaries. Where is the Paris of my mother's
             rebellious cousin who painted with
Max Ernst, or the Paris of my grad student and her new husband,
       noses nuzzling before la tour Eiffel on their
             Facebook post? Or the Paris
of my twenties, when I first floated into Monet's water lilies, when
       the Seine glimmered like a thousand liquid candles

as I sauntered across Pont Marie

at midnight. On l'Avenue de Clichy, on Rue de Rivoli, I see only

dog poop, crumpled plastic bags, and unfiltered

butts. A two-hour wait to enter

Notre Dame, the façade blocked by tawdry bleachers. Pebbles

from the Tuileries have collected in my sandals

though I keep jiggling my feet

to shake them out. Maybe I have actually become my British

uncle. Samuel Johnson said if you're tired

of London, you're tired

of life. I'll bet he'd put Paris in the same category—after all, didn't

he say French faces shine with "a thousand

Graces"? I can't begin to

keep up with my mountain-goat, marathoner husband who'll

cover seven *arrondissements* on foot at

a greyhound's trot. Yet

now, on the day before leaving, I'm fueled by a breakfast of hard

boiled eggs, and he says, how about Sacré Coeur,

it's only a ten-minute walk,

we'll take our time. So we do, and the hill with its rounded, gleaming

white cathedral is washed with breezes. Inside

les Jardins Renoir, we are

alone in the courtyard, red poppies brimming at green edges of

stones, a silence glistening through sudden empty

space. And here it is: not Giverny,

but a round pond, and, *oh! yes!* pink and white water lilies, their

shimmering pads like clean hands open to sky,

stems trailing into the barely

visible muck, and tiny speckled fish burbling to the surface, then

spiraling back down to the silt, murky depths,

the dirt that underlies us all.

from **SHIMMER** (2019)

On the Chinese Scroll

a man in a boat
moves upstream toward
mountains—mist, with his
thin back bent, as he
faces the water
that flows from the hills
to the downstream pool
where he casts his thread-
slender line, alone.

Along a River

you will know upstream
from downstream. Off these
sloped banks, clumped water
hyacinths, mossy
strands provide clues, no
movement other than
scarlet dragonflies
flitting the surface,
mosquitoes. Beyond,
a source you must find.

Maybe His Boat

is drifting back
toward the mouth
of the river,
or he's grown tired
from the long push
and the banks down
farther lure him
with the fine silt
of easy slopes,
silky tendrils,
perhaps under
the mountains' mist
something hides he
fears he will reach.

How a Surface

can gleam in light,
radiant, pure,
a crystalline
slice, so you think
there is no need
to go under.

Even Tarnished

the sterling bowl's
repoussé iris petals swirl

across its rounded center, but
on the base, a crack somewhere,

so water placed inside—to hold
fresh-cut jonquils for a while—

leaks, staining the surface
of a polished table.

The Silver Tongs'

ends are shaped like bay scallops,
whose numbers have diminished in

recent years due to the loss of seagrasses
on which they fastened, and the overfishing of

sharks, who devoured the manta rays that gobbled
the scallops' predators. Such delicate, rounded pincers

are not designed to grasp anything heavier
than a cube of sugar. Scallops: ancient symbol

of the vulva, primal force within the earth. Around
an oval table at dinner, the way a guest's fingers

handled a pair of lustrous tongs could provide
the sterling moment of an evening.

Mom's Creamer

holds only a few
drops, just enough

to soften the bite of over-
steeped lapsang souchong

during late afternoon tea,
which she spent in her final

years alone, unless a daughter
happened to visit. The etched

oval on the side carries no
image—a cameo without

a face. The silver lip of
the creamer angles

to a point, sharp little
beak—peck, peck.

The Dragon Bowl

was the one piece I asked
my sister to send when she decided

to sell all Mom's silver, not because
it was sterling because it wasn't, only plate,

but for the sweeping creature, its tail, spikes,
fangs, claws reaching toward a bulbous sun with

rays that spewed in every direction like the creature
itself spiralling round and round, looping its scaly

body etched and chased across the bowl's width,
this animal whose power for the Chinese lay

in its shedding skin, emerging as a new,
transformed being, able to soar, see

from a great height what has been
and what will come of it.

from **ONE BLACKBIRD AT A TIME** (2015)

I Hate Telling People I Teach English

Like last August, after they'd finished my bone scan,
      this combed-over mid-sixties guy starts chatting about the novel
he's written in his head, he only needs someone like me
      to work it up, he never liked punctuation, parts of speech, all that junk
from junior high, and I couldn't get my print-out fast enough
      to take to my GP, who likes to quote from his inspirational speeches
to local luncheon clubs. He's determined to collect them
      in a book, though he'd need a good editor, do I know any, and meanwhile
I've been waiting fifty-seven minutes for help with recharging
      my sluggish thyroid, and I haven't met any doctors who like giving
free advice about your daughter's milk allergy or your friend's
      migraines or the thumb you slammed in the stairwell door, splitting it
open so badly your students interrupted your lecture on
      pronoun agreement to note you were dripping blood from your hand
and wow, what happened? But it's mostly at parties I hate
      admitting I teach English. I've never been quick enough to fudge,
the way a Methodist minister friend says he's in "support
      services" so he doesn't get called to lead grace. I guess I could dub myself
a "communications facilitator," but since I'm in the business
      of trying to obviate obfuscation, I own up, though I dread what I know
is coming: "Oh," they say, "I hated English, all that grammar,
      you won't like the way I talk, you'll be correcting me," and suddenly
they need another Bud or merlot or they've got to check out
      the meatballs or guacamole over on the table and I'm left facing
blank space, no one who can even think about correcting
      my dangling participles. Once when the computer guy was at the house,
bent over my laptop trying to get us back online,
      he asked what it was I wrote, and when I told him "poetry," said, "Ah—
fluffy stuff," and I wasn't sure whether he was kidding
      or not, but I figured at least it was better than his saying he hated poetry
or that he had a manuscript right outside in his Camry and

could I take a look, no hurry, but he knew it would sell, could I tell him
how to get an agent for his novel about his uncle

moving to Arizona and running a thriving ostrich farm until the day
hot-air balloons took off a half mile away

and stampeded the birds, till all he was left with were feathers and bloody
tangled necks on fence posts, the dream of making two million

from those birds a haunting sentence fragment—but then, I think:
I would never have wanted to miss the time a dentist,

tapping my molars, asked if I'd like to hear him recite Chaucer's Prologue
to *The Canterbury Tales* in Middle English, which he did

while I lay back in his chair, open-mouthed, pierced to the root.

Truth, Beauty, and the Intro Poetry Workshop

Still prickling from a neighbor's yelling "Shove it
                 up your ass" when all I'd done was ask if
       he could stop his terriers
from yapping all night, I wasn't entirely patient when
              the kid with the scarab tattoos effused about
       beauty, said ever since Brit Lit
he's wanted to talk like Milton—"Yet once more, O ye
            Laurels"—or Keats—"Those lips, O slippery
       blisses, twinkling eyes," adding
he's in the class to "build the lofty rhyme." I reminded him
           it's 2010, we don't wear cravats or corsets and
       nobody waltzes anymore. He nodded,
so I asked what music he likes. "Deathcore—It Dies Today
          and Suicide Silence," he said, and then,
       "I'm a drummer." "Aha," I said,
"how about writing a poem the way you wield those sticks." Now
          he's turned in a free-verse sequence leaded
       with expletives about arguments
with his crack-dealing brother who never leaves the house without
         his .38. His lines reverberate with the turbulence
       of a 747 out of LAX. Yet I'm
lashing myself, worrying I did him wrong. I love Auden's
         call to "Let the healing fountain start" from
      "the deserts of the heart,"
but why not water this kid's land-mine-loaded sand
        dunes with a little harmony? The human soul
      needs beauty more
than bread, said Lawrence. Haven't I been yearning for a bit
        of old-school beauty myself? Just last week
    we watched a tennis princess
swear she'd take her fuckin' ball and slam it down the fuckin'
      judge's throat. I know poetry's got to breathe
    with the fumes of its time,
but I'd like to escape my own, forget about drugged-up

kids with guns. And it isn't even true nobody
waltzes anymore. How
could I have forgotten that night downtown a year ago
when, as the symphony in the outdoor pavilion
lilted into "The Blue Danube,"
a thousand people all joined in, arms lifting to arms,
lovers and uncles, grandmas and bikers, moms
and toddlers dancing
under the moon to soaring melodies barely heard these days,
till we became one rhapsodic, dactylic swirl.

Waking over *Call It Sleep*

I'm the closest thing to Jewish in the class even though
at best I'm only one-eighth, according
     to my English mother, who insisted the shadowy figure
of her granny was a Jew since nobody knew
     her origins and everybody talked as if something had been
hushed up, shameful, and of course
     everything about her hawk-nosed face was unusually dark,
especially the ringlets of her unruly hair,
     or I suppose you could count the fact that I'm married
to a man whose grandparents arrived
     at Ellis Island from what is now Ukraine only three years
after Henry Roth, yet none of these
     students has the *sekhl* to know their teacher is a *shiksa*
and our group is as goyish as pork chops
     but they've all been children, and they love this novel,
they know what it's like to be
     speechless, powerless, afraid. Nobody needs me to explain
the terror of what lies beyond
     the front door and what lies within, and the paralysis
that comes from never knowing
     when to dash outside or stand by the window behind
the blinds. One year, while we were reading
     Ginsberg, I knew I'd have to describe Kaddish
though I'd never even heard it
     recited, but I gave it a go, saying in passing that only
1% of our city's population is Jewish
     which was when Heather quipped: "Of course, they're all
in Hollywood making millions from
     trashy movies." I put down my book and didn't move—
you could hear the whirr
     of the elevator down the hall. When I spoke, I said, "That

was a *very* offensive comment"—and

     I realized I was shaking, after decades of holding forth
in linoleum-floored classrooms. It wasn't

     like the times I've heard someone saying *wet* meaning
wetback which are both despicable

     terms and I argue those too, but this time it was as if
I'd been slapped full in the face, called

     sheeny, kike, and I swear that tears came to my eyes though
I couldn't cry out "*Gevalt,* help,

     take that back, you ignorant little bitch." The tension lasted
beyond the ten-minute break, which

     I loosened to twenty, and not just for the smokers. Now
I've handed out maps that highlight

     Galicia, Brooklyn, Tysmenicz, the Lower East Side,
Avenue D, and 9th Street, and a list with

     explanations of terms: Passover, Ashkenazi, knish, shul,
and pogrom. We talk about Friday night

     and the candles, and everyone is right there in the room
with Roth and with me and with my husband

     who joins us after the break to tell about the author's
life with his duck farm and his goyish wife

     and his writer's block, and I begin to wonder if any of these
students with family from Monterrey or

     Laredo will some day learn—as a friend of mine did last year—
that a great-great-great-and-beyond

     grandfather came over from Spain to escape the Inquisition,
and if it will happen—as my friend Raúl

     told me it did—that in the lighting of candles with relatives
gathered for a first Shabbat, an elderly aunt

     in the corner will begin to sigh and to weep, and when they
press her, ask her what's wrong,

she'll tell them she's suddenly remembering an abuela
who covered her face with her hands
      every Friday night to greet the Divine, the Shekhinah,
and who every week sent one grandchild
      to buy candles. A child, I'm thinking, who wore a silver
cross around her neck and had never
      heard *judía de mierda* hurled in her face with the auto-pilot
contempt of the six girls who chanted
      at me in the bathroom once during second grade, as they
pointed at the color of my striped
      dress: "Blue, blue, you're a Jew," but I didn't get it—
I thought they were saying *jewel.*

Books, Bath Towels, and Beyond

After Gary asked "Will we ever read
        any normal people in this class?" and I quipped,
                "No, of course not," and after the laughter had quieted,
we ambled through "Song of Myself," celebrating
        our "respiration and inspiration," traveling along
                with the voices of sailors, prostitutes, presidents, and tree-toads,
in sync with the poet's vision. No one
        this time—not even Gary—grumbled about
                Whitman's disgusting ego, and yet when we came to the place
where God is "a loving bedfellow"
        who leaves "baskets covered with white towels
                bulging the house with their plenty," I was the one who
wanted to stop. At that point, I've always
        been puzzled. I get it that a lover could
                be like a god. But *towels*? We'd just finished *The House
of the Seven Gables*, and I wondered if
        Hepzibah or Phoebe ever sold linens in their shop. Yet
                we never hear Hawthorne talking about blankets or sheets or
how anybody washes his face or her hands,
        let alone armpits or "soft-tickling genitals"—leave
                those to Uncle Walt. The store Hepzibah opened: a first step
in leaving the shadows of her cursed
        ancestors, of joining the sunlit world. Last summer
                when my husband and I moved back into our old house after
a massive redo, we gave away box after box
        of sweaters and tchotchkes. We even disposed of old
                books, including those with my neon markings in the margins
blunt as Gary's outbursts in class: "Ugh,"
        "NO," and "Wow!" It was time to loosen the mind
                beyond the nub of the old self. My mother used to huff through
the house every year like a great wind,

and when she settled down, not a doll over

       twelve months old remained, not a dress, not a scarf, not even

lint wisping in a drawer. One year during

    a flood, my husband's letters from lifelong friends

       drowned in the garage, morphed back into pulp. I never hoped

the past would vanish into a blank, and yet,

    when Holgrave in the novel cries, "Shall we never,

       never get rid of this Past!" I, too, want it washed clean, to wake

in the morning released from echoes

    of my father's muttered invectives, my mother's

       searing tongue. I've now torn to rags the rust-stained towels

from my former marriage and

    my husband's bachelorhood linens, raveled

       threads drooping like fishnets. How Hawthorne's Phoebe

opened that heavy-lidded house

    to the light. I used to scorn her chirpy domesticity,

       praying along with Emily Dickinson—whose balance

Gary had also questioned—"God keep me

    from what they call *households*." And yet, after

       my husband and I returned to our remade, renewed house,

what did I do but go shopping

    for towels. Back and forth to seven strip malls,

       bringing home only to return I don't know how many colors,

till finally, I settled on white. And as I

    pulled out my MasterCard to pay for the contents of

       my brimming cart, a gaunt wrinkled man entered the check-out

line, hands pressing to his chest

    two white towels just like mine, eyes lifted

       to the fluorescent ceiling as if in prayer. I doubt that Gary

would think it normal to greet the divine

    while clutching terry cloth. But now I see that Whitman

knew what fresh towels could mean for a dazed and puffy
face, white towels unspecked by blood
      or errant coils of hair, towels that spill from
            a laundry basket like sea-foam. Like cirrus clouds adrift while
we're loafing on tender, newly sprouted
      blades of grass growing from the loam under our boot soles,
         from graves of the old and decaying, all we've finally buried.

About That "One Art"

It's a perfect poem, I say, and though no one
                    in the class is over twenty-five, everybody
nods. They've all lost: the Madame
                    Alexander doll fallen into the toilet, silky
hair never the same, the friend who
                    moved away to Dallas, a brother once again
in juvie. So many schools—thirteen in
                    a dozen years—I lost each friend I made
till grad school. And every move since,
                    something always missing—this last time,
the box that held my photo albums
                    of the sixties, that elastic, unveined life I'd
love to visit just once more. And now
                    the husbands of so many have diminished—
the cancerous prostates, the double
                    bypasses, the radiation, the chemo. One died
while napping. And how many women friends
                    have lost a breast? Or two? Now I wonder,
who'll be leaving first: me, or you? Just how
                    will that be mastered? And how is it even time
begins to lose itself? In class I ask why Bishop
                    wrote the poem as a villanelle, and so we
parse the form, say how such echoing
                    slows us, keeps us focused on each single
disappearance, so at first we hear lightheartedness,
                    a witty irony—but then the sounds grow
vaster, catch us off guard. And quicken.

Teaching *Mrs. Dalloway* I'm Thinking

How I'd like to buy flowers, how I'd like to place a sterling
     silver bowl of peonies or cut-glass vase of tulips and irises
on the laminate seminar table in this windowless room,
     and I'm thinking how I'd like to arrive before the one student
always a half-hour early, how I'd like to greet each of them
     at the door, inquire after their sisters and cousins, their tíos
and abuelitas, and comfort the one who's been fired
     from his job. Every Tuesday another novel about the modern
condition, those catchy phrases we use: "alienation
     and fragmentation"—while for the past three weeks Jill,
the debate team captain on two scholarships, hasn't said
     a word because, she told me sobbing at the break, her boyfriend
was found bloody in his apartment, shot by her brother
     off his meds, and Angie, dispatching for Pleasure U Hot Line,
her shift moved to graveyard, slumps dozing
     in her chair. Now Jeffrey is saying, "She's snobbish, Clarissa,
I don't like her, who cares about her maids and
     her flowers, but she's right, I mean, she gets it, nothing like
a great party." It's the dinner hour, though no bells chime
     on this campus, and only two of us have actually heard Big Ben,
have ever strolled through Regent's Park, ridden on
     a red double-decker. But nobody around this table wonders
why Septimus hurls himself out the window, nobody
     needs PTSD explained, and when Marita asks, "Wasn't it Woolf
who filled her pockets with stones and walked into
     a river?" nobody says "weird," their two dozen heads bent over
pages littered with post-its. I'm thinking how I want
     to say something, mend this rent in the air the way Clarissa
gathers the raveled threads of her ripped dress with a needle,
     the way she draws everyone into her party, but already it's time

to pack up our pens, our notebooks, head out on the crowded
      interstate, past all the newly constructed buildings with no
balconies, no wrought iron railings, these multiple stories
      of steel and glass, mirrored so no one can see into them.

Langston Hughes' "Weary Blues"

Needs no explaining in this class. No one needs a gloss

on "Suicide's Note," that river so calm, asking a kiss,

yet none of us around this table

has ever been kept out of a KFC or a multiplex

because of our skin. "Nobody knows the trouble

I've seen," sang Lena Horne, who couldn't stay

at the Savoy-Plaza after she'd

made the crowd swing. Enough trouble right here

in this room. Ann's just driven from the hospice,

her gay dad's body shriveling into the sheets,

her mother and brothers refusing

to visit. Last week Robert's cousins were found

mangled by the train tracks in Sabinas for the Los Zetas

dope they were running, only way to pay for beans

and rice. This morning in my office

Christina soaked through the six tissues I offered

as she told how the fucked-up ex-marine raped her

in the ass over and over, his loaded .45 beside

the pillow. No wonder Hughes'

pianist "stopped playing and went to bed," where

he "slept like a rock or a man that's dead." I need

to focus on the poem, call and response, structure

of the blues. Nathan might help,

he's a musician. But already he's talking: "Hey, after

class, how many of y'all want to drive over to JJ's, awesome

piano, sax, bass." And all I say is, "Count me in."

I'm Not Sure the Cherry Is the "Loveliest of Trees"

So from the first line of the poem I'm quibbling,
                    and I don't even teach this poem now
I'm pushing threescore and ten. All that counting
                    Housman has us busy doing, figuring
the speaker's age, and I know in class we'd end up
                    focusing on the stanzas with the math. Yet
students never had trouble getting hold
                    of the poem's carpe diem message: Inhale
the scent of roses while you can. I've never seen
                    a flowering cherry, have never known
spring in Washington D.C. or England or
                    been invited to a hanami, a party to view
the blooms in Tokyo. But I knew the dogwoods
                    lacing my first hesitant steps, have known
white pines' needles gleaming with
                    light reflected from a northern lake, and
I've known the palo verdes in the dusty Sonoran
                    desert where Rudy, my first boyfriend,
kissed me. And the olives I planted
                    with my former husband, shoveling down
into Phoenix hardpan. The eucalyptus lifting
                    their astringent scent in the Berkeley hills
where I lay in a carpet of fog-softened leaves, ecstatic
                    with a lover. The lemon tree by the front door
of the house where my son was born. I could say
                    "with rue my heart is laden" for these and all
the trees I may never see again: banyans and teak,
                    neem trees, cinnamon and coconut palms,
the bodhi tree—under which the Buddha
                    sat so still. And since I haven't many springs

like the woman diagnosed with terminal
cancer who traveled seven continents
compiling a life list of eight thousand birds,
I could search out all the trees I've never seen,
including the blossoming cherry. In California
there's a bristlecone that's lived for almost
five thousand years, and in Sweden, a spruce
that's lived for close to ten. That woman's travels
kept her cancer in remission, her doctors
were amazed. But how can I leave our own
Mexican persimmon near the drive, its peeling
layers of coppery silver bark, its branching
trunk I can't begin to wrap my arms around?

Arriving at Wallace Stevens in the 13th Week

      I borrow an apple from Amy, place it on the carpet, and ask
what's changed, as we stare at this red and yellow
      freckled luminescence, our circled desks surrounding the mind
of nothing in our midst, altered by the various
      blues of our various guitars. We agree "Study of Two Pears"
is about pears, but "The Idea of Order at Key West"
      hums beyond the genius of these walls, and twenty pairs of eyes
puzzle over wide-open Nortons till Tony proclaims
      the singer in the poem to be the moon, since it's always pulling
at the tides, causing the ocean's roar. But
      tonight I stifle my irritation that he's found what isn't there
in the poem's portrayal of a woman's seaside
      singing. For once I let Tony be artificer of his own notes,
even if dimly starred, as he strides alongside
      the poem, thwarting my blessed rage for order honed by forty
years in classrooms. Yet I want him to slip
      barefoot into the poem's curling surf, want him to swim out
into the noctilucent swell of it with no guiding moon
      or pinpoint of harbor light, just the rise and fall of the waves
with their unpredictable lines, the undertow
      of the water's elastic weight, though I don't want him to drown,
and maybe I'm the one who's deaf to songs
      along the shore, to hymns that buzz beside my ears. Maybe
I can follow only one blackbird at a time,
      blind to the undulate spangles of another's sense of things.

The Last Time I Taught Robert Frost

I shuddered when Olivia, who is writing her dissertation
            on dialectics of the self in Gloria Anzaldúa, announced she found him
lovely. "Lovely?" I cried, professional composure shot,
            my image of Frost collapsing suddenly as the Great Stone Face
on Cannon Mountain, the craggy Old Man fallen in shards
            to the ground. True, this was not on par with the vandalizing
of his house in Vermont, Homer Noble Farm's wicker chairs,
            wooden tables, dressers smashed and thrown into the fire to keep
the place warm while thirty kids swilled a hundred and fifty
            cans of Bud with a dozen bottles of Jack Daniel's, and threw up
on the floor. After all, Olivia wasn't saying she didn't like
            the poems, but *lovely*? A word my mother detested as phony,
like someone holding a pinkie straight out while drinking tea,
            the sort of word my grandmother used when vaguely praising
a Bartók piece, or a play she didn't understand. Like people
            saying, "How interesting," when what they really mean is, "Spare me
the details," or, "Could we change the subject." So when
            I asked Olivia what she meant by "lovely" and she talked about
the lush, long vowel sounds, I wondered why I'd felt stabbed,
            until I remembered my father's lying in the ICU, the fat respirator
tube jammed down his throat, the whoosh of forced breath
            fogging the glassed-in-room, and my stroking his forehead while
my father, whom I'd never seen cry, began to leak tears down
            his chiseled face. Finally, not knowing what more to do, I stood
by the window staring out at the New Hampshire pines
            and began reciting one of his favorite poems: "I must go down
to the seas again, to the lonely sea and the sky." He started
            to jerk, whole body spasms under the sheets, more tears carving
runnels down his cheeks, and I knew he wanted me to recite
            "Stopping By Woods," his most-loved poem and maybe mine too,

but I couldn't. I couldn't turn from that window looking

out at the trees beyond the parking lot, the words to the one
poem I've known by heart for decades buried somewhere

below my throat. He died the next day. Maybe that was why
I asked the class if we could recite it, if perhaps some of them

even had it memorized, and Denise and Lupe and Nathaniel actually
said they had. So we chanted it, the other eight of us

reading from the Norton's crisp, white pages, but when we came
to the ending, not a single student needed to look down

as we sang the last stanza all together. I can't explain it, but for once
something dark and deep entered among us in the overly

air-conditioned room. As if we were all one self and yet still alone
in the cold, and wanting to stay. When we spoke again,

we talked until I had to stand up, open the door, and tell them
to leave, say it was past time for their dinners and

all the lovely, nagging promises waiting for them to keep.

from **FROM THE MOON, EARTH IS BLUE** (2015)

Closeted Indigo

It's the full moon we notice, not the night sky.
The white cat, not the shadowed grass.

Almost invisible, slipped between blue
and violet: Newton sensed it was there.

A color is only waves, motion we can't hear.
Veins near the skin run blue, bleed red.

We barely see the blueberries plucked in the night
silence when a loon cries on the lake.

There are ways of bludgeoning so the bruises
don't show, closets with walls no one can see.

It's the light glinting on leaf shapes
that dazzles us, the shimmers on the river.

What color is the wail of a horn uncoiled,
a saxophone's moan through the door?

Apologia for Brown

"A good picture, like a good fiddle, should be brown."
—Sir George Beaumont

Half light, candle light, window
to a street awash with slop.
Sienna, ochre, burnt umber,
Cassel earth derived from peat.
Bister: soot from birch bark.

Roof and mantel, fallow field and
pumpernickel (a word formed
from "pumpern," "fart"), roasted
beef, saddle and shoe, potato skin.
Pitchy murk they dug from soil.

Least glamorous of pigments.
The impressionists got rid of it.
Oozings of the lower gut,
a meaty sauce, a sobering glaze.
Caravaggio, Rembrandt, Van Dyck.

Eyes looking out like inner
rings within the cores of trees.
Hard maple, spruce, carved and
varnished till a violinist draws
a horsehair-fitted bow across

the belly of an instrument
that, strung in those days with
the dried intestines of a sheep,
might, even now, wrench us
beyond our fetid rooms,

the way a spotted moth will cling,
a dark stain, to the wall of the garage,
till it wafts its small
hand's width of weightlessness
through transparent air.

Composition in Gray

Dust to dust, but it's not that: dirt is yellow, brown, or red.
Ashes, not even that, for these are also chunks of bone.

Desaturated light, the volume turned below our vision.
Her pulse at twelve, then under seven beats a minute.

Throat-choking fog through night and noon, a pall that blurs
angles of walls, the street signs turned to fuzz, illegible.

Our senses can't discern the subtler shades
of avian plumage, the various grays on chickadees.

Not even that. As though her ashes in the jar had drifted out
and, lofted by the air, have sifted over everything.

And now the lake has died, the parasites, giardia, the scum
of algae multiplied, loons abandoning their nests.

Buried within the Munsell Color System's inner core,
achromatic, oxymoron, color of no color.

And still she stares at us from photographs.
A cinema in black and white, continuously reeling.

At the end, I stroked her toes, bare of their familiar polish.
Within the room, not even shadows, even shade.

Apology for Blue

"Don't prate to me of divinity . . . but of blue."
—William Gass

A form of black, said the Greeks,
cousin of gray, species
of darkness, opposite of light,
not a mention in Homer
with his wine-dark seas.

Even the Bible doesn't note
the celestial vault is blue.
We've three times more synonyms
for red—cerulean lacks
the force of blood's vermilion.

And yet Cennini's quattrocento
brought back lapis lazuli
from Badakshan, ground
the heavy, gray-veined stone
to paste, kneaded it like bread,

sieved, melted, strained the stuff
through linen, then mixed in lye
and slapped the lump with sticks
till the blue drained off, a powder
stored in a leather purse.

Reserved for the Virgin's lap.
Color of meekness and profound
piety, the heavenly spirit,
that woman's body cool,
unsullied by carnality, wrapped in

blue more dear than gold.
But nineteenth-century scientists
observed, in the Bunsen burner's
flame, the highest heat is blue.

The hottest stars are bluish white,

and objects hurtling near light speed
show bluer than the slower ones—
in physics, blue's the color
of collision, fire, the laser's beam
that centuries of artists showed

streaming to a mortal woman's lap:
fulcrum of our heated lives,
hinge and spring of our renewal.
Hard to see what's closest.
From the moon, earth is blue.

High Yellow

(Ellsworth Kelly, Oil on canvas, 1960, Blanton Museum of Art)

This is it. All you need. Though nothing
resembles anything you know. It's neither
star nor flower, this imperfect oval more
like a fat yellow cigar floating in blue so dark
and bright it couldn't be any sky that's ever
filled your breath. And the bottom third
of the canvas: pure green. You don't have
to do a thing. Can stop the churning of your
desire to turn this high-flying ovoid into an
ear of corn or a squashed halo. This is only
about color: yellow, blue, green. But your
mind is still recalling that the first two can
make the third. Like sun and sky make grass.
You keep trying to put names on these three
shapes, though they have nothing to do with
names. Yet you can't leave, for in the high
sky above this bright lawn, a widening sun is
about to drop the egg of itself into your lap.

from **NOTHING BETWEEN US** (2009)

Teaching *Uncle Tom's Children*

He was the only other honky in the room. But wasn't. Blond natural. Was his mother or his dad White or Black? Kid played the best sax in town and only fourteen. Sax so sweet and cool the moon rose cream over the hills and stars broke the fog. He didn't talk much. Neither did I, that first Black Lit class any of us taught. I didn't know what to put on the board. Erased everything I'd written before, but the erasers were full of dust from the chalk. The blackboard turned powdery, a blur, clouded. We moved on through *Nigger, Black Boy, Native Son*. Not a kid caused trouble. Small sounds, fingers flipping the white pages of the paperbacks I collected and stacked in the corner cupboard after class. Slap of gum stretching in and out of a mouth, hard sole of a shoe on the floor, scraping the surface, an emery board. And the train, track barely a block away, the train running the whole length of the San Francisco Bay, cry moving ahead of it, toward us, that wail.

Folks

I didn't know what I'd been doing wrong in the Track 2 class. Till one of the counselors told me to stop saying *folks*. Not a friendly word, especially since the assassinations, Martin Luther King and Malcolm. Almost as bad as *coloreds*, *nigras*. Didn't even realize I'd been saying it— okay folks, time to get out your pencils. Thought of it as a neighborly word, an offering, sort of like a covered dish at a potluck. A long way from my own folks in Phoenix. Family. During that first semester James Carmichael would stay after second period and help straighten the desks. Don't you worry Miss, he'd say, they'll most of them be fine. Just take them a little time to get used to you.

One Friday around the middle of October, Calvin Jones cussed so much in class I led him out to the hall and leaned into his face: look at me, look me in the eyes when I'm talking to you. At lunch the other teachers told me he was just being polite—you looked down, showed respect, never looked straight into the eyes of your teacher, especially your white teacher, especially your white woman teacher.

It was later in the year that James Carmichael joined the Black Muslims. New black slacks and tie, stiff white shirt. He'd been right, most everybody, even Calvin, had come around. But James had stopped smiling, his eyes gone somewhere else. He still turned in his work on time, still made B's. But there was nothing between us, never had been.

Audio Visual

One of the boys would help if the film broke. Some of them even knew how to fix the oldest projector, the one that sputtered and cluttered and moaned to a stop in the middle of the story. Like when Ulysses had himself bound up, so he could sail past the sirens, or when he was barely making it through between Scylla and Charybdis. A couple of the girls would stay and talk over their sandwiches at lunchtime about Mr. Taylor who always asked for help in the auditorium's projection booth whenever they showed movies for all the history classes at once. He'd accidentally brush against them in the dark, then take his time feeling them up. They laughed about it. Everybody thought he was pretty cute. The administrators had their eye on him to get his credential, be a principal in a year or two. Movie days were a relief. The sound drowned out the traffic on University Avenue, and even late in the afternoon, with the blinds down the pimps didn't bother to hassle their girls through the windows, hollering in, *Inetta, you get your black ass out on this street, Yvonne, you hear me girl.* Even with the volume turned up high, the sound track distorted, everything seemed just that much quieter.

Macramé

I never got into it. Too many knots. Rope or string, mostly white, or that pale yellowy color, twisted in on itself, maybe a few beads. All that work just to hold a house plant off the floor. I was weaving. Different yarns. Crinkly silk, like hair from an unraveled braid. Silver. A fat wool, furry, the shade of lichen under a pine. And blue, a deep teal, turquoise, the way you remember an inland high sky in winter. Purple, fuchsia, orange, sunsets. Dawn. Sometimes I thought of the students I liked while I worked. Frances, her low voice, her cello. Jennifer's little giggles. Charles, his wide smile, giant Afro. Andrew, trying to get me to read *Dune*. The warp strands sturdy, brown. Backstrap loom tied to the window latch. I pushed the weft threads down, a soft thud. Over and under. One color showing more now, another the next time. I gathered eucalyptus bells that fell under the tall trees in the hills. Clean-smelling, a good medicine. I liked working the dark seeds into the pattern. I wanted to make something big, fill a space, soften a wall.

On the Bay

It was the art teacher Norm who had the doctor friend who was leasing the twenty-seven-foot sailboat we took out onto the bay that Saturday before Margie the history teacher's party and we smoked dope all day on the water. There for a while we drifted out beyond the Golden Gate into the open sea before we knew what we were doing so it took about three hours just to get back under the bridge, everybody laughing except the one guy who'd had the six sailing lessons so he knew what was maybe about to happen. Norm was getting it on with Nini on the foam mattress under the prow and everybody else was sopping from the spray that was everywhere over us. That whole day no fog at all, even after we docked back at the Marina and stopped at the Safeway to pick up some Cribari red for the party where Margie had put out candles on the tables, all sizes and shapes burning down puddles of different colors of hot wax around their flames like the lights of the city we'd just spent the whole day sailing past, turned on.

Freed up

He said I had nice ones, even though I'd always thought they were so little, but why did I bind them up? One day I left my bra in the drawer. All day could feel the feel of them. Couldn't forget they were there. Felt good just leaning down to throw a wad of paper in the trash. And standing up, nipples like third and fourth eyes, looking straight out at whoever was coming toward me in the long hall. Looking clear inside. Into secrets, hiding places. Until they were out for good, out of the muffled fiber-filled shells, elastic tightenings, hard-wire frames. Like bare green leaves unfolding in April, swelling as they opened. Leisurely, soft, brushing into a hand.

Integration

Almost lost in his mouth. He'd told me I didn't know how to kiss, I was trying too hard, and showed me, so our mouths ripened to plush opening peonies, ruffling, even a bit messy at the edges. More than a mother's mouth, nipple, these kisses. Shape to shape, unforming and reshaping, play of inner cheek and tongue. My consonants: so crisp, he said. Every one of my syllables clear, enunciated. But this now was a time for vowels, color, the fibrous textures of slow dipthongs, blurred edges letting *is* blend into *us*, long *es* open into *ah, o, oh, oh, oh*.

Sax

Cool slow riff, under, over, around and around one central note that took a long time to find. The sheets ruffled across the bed and down, spread like a fan, a loose shawl. Wet spot dry now. Sprawled pages of the paper. Fog breezing into the window over the bed. His arms. Warm. As if I were wrapped in my own little girlhood, cradled for Vespers in my granddad's boat, oars shipped, stilled in the shallows of the evening lake as the singing began on shore, *carry me home, coming for to carry me*. All the notes of those voices. Ripples of the water, colors of pearl in the darkening, boat rocking. The wide water. Then back across, oars dripping, across the lake to sleep, in the long quiet of the night. Until waked by a cry coming from the center of silence, loon call, tremolo rising across the brush-tops of the pines in the blackness. Joined, by another, and another, by another.

Half and Half

I'd eaten less and less, no carbohydrates, mainly protein, hard-boiled eggs. At first I thought the school I'd been assigned to was ninety percent black. Naturals swirled black halos around me till even at home at night I thought I would disappear. By Halloween I knew it was more like half and half. That was around the time I heard the whispering outside my classroom door after everyone else had gone home, felt afraid as I had during the riots in South Side Chicago. The whisperings grew louder, what they would do to me. I stood up from my desk and walked right past them and down the hall to the principal's office before I started to cry.

All this was before Ty was there. Nobody knew, and we made sure we kept it that way, but I could think about him all day and at night, about the way his darkness slid right into me, how he filled me with himself until I felt I'd split open.

One Saturday night when I didn't go home, I stared for a long time at his one poster hanging on the wall. A little black boy dressed in white and sitting in a white chair in a room with white walls, white ceiling, and a white floor. Sometime in the night I started to shiver, cold without a nightgown. I was half asleep when he went to the closet, pulled down a brown wool blanket. From his mother, he said, when he left Georgia to play for Colorado. And he'd needed all the warm blankets he could get in Boulder, those high white mountains. He made sure I was covered up before he lay down again next to me. Sweet smell of his hair. In the morning I didn't want to leave. He brought the donuts into bed, the kind with the soft cream filling. That was when he told me where the scars on his shoulders came from. If you ever have a son, he said, don't let him play football. You can get torn up, bad, before your time.

Luminous

Luminous was the word he used. Repeated it. Yeah, he said, that's it, that's what you are. Luminousness. Each syllable a slow mouthful. Luminescence. His tongue and lips made full contact with every consonant, as if he were walking deliberately through a dark, vacant room, turning on all the lamps. But I never told him how even before he opened the door to my classroom, I would know. A quiet grew behind the clanging of lockers, the hollered motherfuckers. A soft silence that had nothing to do with speechlessness. The volume just turned itself down. Even in the middle of the hall's screeching at second lunch (*where you think you be walking to, honky bitch*) he brought with him a thick-carpeted room of sleek and steady upholstery, padded back and arms of a good chair. No fear of a lamp's being toppled, or the cord yanked.

Remedial Reading

The smallest classroom in the ninth-grade school. Yellow walls, and the ceiling seemed too high. Boxes lined up in bright colors on the tables, each a different level. This class for retards? This a toony class? The kids swaggered and straggled through the door, unwilling. To be seen here. Laminated cards, one at a time. Second-, third-grade skills for fourteen-year- olds. Mostly boys. I'd been assigned to help the reading teacher, her thick gray hair bunched and slipping along with hairpins and combs. Ruth organized field trips, took her own beat-up station wagon. Once she drove us up the coast to the great blue herons' nesting grounds. We walked up and up until we could look straight down into the tops of the big trees. She showed us how to spot the saucers of nests resting in the branches.

I never got the kids to move beyond a level or two. Nobody stayed on task. Once I was pronouncing vowels with Lester Sims, light-skinned, freckled, a skinny little dude. *O: okra, Oakland, Coke. And o: butter, supper, dove.* His eyes shone. He was standing beside me. Doves, he said. We can talk about birds? Sure, I said, and told him about the finches I was raising at home in as big a cage as I could afford. Man, why didn't you say you wanted us to talk about birds? And he was out the door. Before the bell rang for the next class he was back. I was putting cards away in their boxes, red tipped ones in the red box, brown in brown, folding the lids closed. You like pigeons? he grinned. I do, I do, I said. He unzipped his jacket. I don't know how many wings flapped out from him, ruffled my hair and fluttered all through that yellow room, a sound only feathers can make, as Lester told me every one of their names.

from **THINGS OF THE WEATHER** (2008)

Contrails

Lines that reverberate
beyond the actor's exit.
A bite embedded,
burr in a bermuda lawn.
An enemy's position
can be calculated
from a plane's traces.
The exhalations freeze
as they leave the tail,
it's ice crystals we see
as a trail of tissue,
nail clippings, a snake skin
the plane has moved beyond.
But sometimes the lines
retain their sharp edges
and criss-cross above
like blades slashing
the last word.

Stratus Opacus Nebulosus

Not a verb in sight,
the train blocking
miles of traffic, no end
to these errands, piles
of provisions, necessary
comestibles, heavy sacks,
a vegetable persistence.

Thunder

To Descartes, one cloud falling
onto another. To the Greeks,
Zeus's shield shaking, a forerunner
of Hopkins' shook foil, that grandeur,
gathered and charged. For the native
tribes of the plains, Thunderbird's
wings beating. Such magnified
oscillations are beyond us, yet
the very air we breathe is grumbling,
a succession of compressions,
negative and positive ions colliding,
as someone in the next room
is about to explode.

Cumulous and Cirrus

About such majesty
they were dead on, those Old
Masters of the page-long
paragraph with parentheticals,
semi-colons, punctuation
marks as spirals, curlicues,
and always, the light
behind the foaming flesh
of turbulence, perhaps
even a god in the air.

from **BETWEEN FRAMES** (2006)

Trash

"Trash," he said, as we walked the line
between our almost-country properties.
Again I pointed, trees and shrubs
whose names I didn't know, but "trash,"
he said again. Anything not oak.

That neighbor knew three kinds of trees:
live, pin, and Spanish oak. The rest should go.
And now I've lived here twenty years
I know how chainsaws take out everything
that isn't oak, not just the junipers

that choke the other plants nearby, but also
Texas buckeyes, magenta blooming in
the spring, redbuds, huisachillo, sweet acacia.
Mexican persimmon's bark blends velvet
grays and silky browns, its rounded leaves

bright yellow-green before the purple fruit
draws birds that nest on into June—
buntings and the wrens above the grasses,
gramas and the bluestems. November,
the seed heads in waves of burgundy, of red.

Our city council said they'd leave the trees
when clearing for the city hall. But like
that neighbor years ago, they meant
the oaks. Now they've called a meeting.
Oak wilt has hit the neighborhood, and

oaks are what we're left with. Too much
construction, trimming of the trees, their
wounds not treated. The virus travels
through the maze of connecting roots.
And once a tree's infected, it's trash.

Reflection

Massacre in Kosovo, but I
am folding blankets on our bed,
nap of the wool, weave over weave

neat and ready for sleep after
the ten o'clock news: homes blazing
raw-boned to blackened skies, smoke

mingling with cloud—or is it
fog? Nothing blurs these
dislocated faces. Last summer

in the flood friends lost their home
of thirty years, everything downhill.
I've started folding the towels.

Lengthwise, in half, and again.
Outside in this morning light
the male cardinal cheeps in pyracantha

at the window. Flitting, as if ready to nest,
but we haven't spotted his mate.
All last year we woke to her beak

attacking the bedroom window. Over
and over, the glass rattling our heads.
She began at daylight, broke our dreams.

I've heard they die
that way, not knowing it's only
a mirror, a reflection of themselves.

from **POEMS FROM PARADISE** (2005)

Lemon, Oak, Cypress

But there were so many others,
leaves like new lace,
fine crochet, and so many
kinds of seeds—round, like bells,
butterflies, or birds' wings.
And the trees with the big leaves,
the leaves, like your hands.

The Third Week

I noticed the orchids,
petals, calyx, and called,
and you said yes, yes,
but it was the water you saw,
streams, both sides of the path.

What you loved—and what
we looked at for a long
time—was the dark water
beside the pale orchids,
the steady, even flow of it.

Once

the scent of jasmine sifted
air, there was no moving

back, no turning from the sway
of stem, petal, trunk,

till neither of us could
stay upright. Leaning, dropping

to the softest grasses,
how strange that afterward

we simply rose. Was it
jasmine that blended us

into these intricate twinings?
And such a tiny blossom.

Whether

one of us breathed
the sky or skimmed

lake shimmer, we didn't
ask of light that wove us,

keel and pool, air
and water. We never

asked if one of us
was an illusion.

We lived as the calla
lily's tongue lies

embedded in the creamy
bloom, full sail.

Butterfly

After, we lay still, our backs
in touch as if we had

become one body.
Our heads, knees resting

on the ground, leaned
to either side, wings, readying

for the flight ahead.
We did not think in halves.

If a God

comes to you
a small
fish in the night,
simply
become water.

∞

If a dove drifts
under your sheets
let him stay,
tuck his head
in a soft place,
rest, until
you are feathers.

∞

He may come
as a lizard, a slip
of a green
slither across
your wall, crevices
left from past
freezes and thaws,
as he turns
translucent, persimmon,
ablaze.

∞

Or a monkey,
who leaps
your crenelations.
Weightless
motion of silver-
brown fur, uncurling
tail, and keen
eyes focused
in, beyond.

∞

When a god comes
to you as a man,
you will have no need
for questions, blossoms,
or bracelets.
Even a name.

from WAY OF WHITENESS (2000)

Taking a Language

I hear them, my husband and son, practicing
sounds in French I have almost forgotten.

La famille. Leurs mots. Deux, trois.
I don't join them. I have enough to do.

Every day the same steps to another day,
blinds pulled until the metal slats slide

to a tidy line above the window.
One bed made at a time, one side at a time,

my arms not long enough
to cross the space between us.

I have grown impatient with slow
progressions—with touch that may not lead

to love, the time it takes
to wait for the ends of sentences—and yet

in high school we couldn't even complete
a simple Latin sentence as

we followed our teacher through each
person of a verb, singular, *amo, amas, amat,*

plural, *amamus, amatis, amant,* present, past,
future perfect conditional.   We didn't know

where we were going. I had no idea
in that class I would meet the boy whose

tongue was the first to reach to mine.
It took our entire sophomore year to translate

Caesar's accounts of the individual
customs of the tribes, the Helvetii, Belgae.

All Gaul was divided into single parts.
Evenings facing a new grammar,

nights in the back seat of a Chevy,
years before we were proficient

in the language of the country of love,
before we had entered

a French cathedral, to find the pattern
of small stones lined

to lead the devout to a state of prayer. Placing
the left foot one stone in front of the right,

heel and sole on stone,
one does not notice the rose window above

until, with an accidental glance,
light explodes, wheeling

spheres within spheres,
mother, child, man, innumerable

facets of glass. I had forgotten.
And below, a smaller window

where shoemakers bend to their task,
to draw the laces through,

one, two at a time.

Some Days the Only

horse in the field is the dull gray one.
Days when a husband of many years sags

into the upholstery of what might have been.
Days when I stare beyond his head

to relive the moments I have said no
to say yes to the familiar, keep intact

the tidiness of cupboards. For years
I have been sweeping, vacuuming dust

that refuses to settle. Even the grasses
of the field have turned drab as the horse,

beyond whose bulk may be nothing, not even
a gate leading to winter ground.

Of Mice and Men

1.

We are setting traps, packs of d-Con. Overrun
again by mice, rolls of paper towels chewed through,
soft nests of leavings
over the floor, bits of bird seed,
clumps of the litter left after the hamster died.

So old he could no longer move to his water.
You drowned him, our fourth hamster.
We decided not to replace him.

We set bait in every kitchen cupboard.
By the third morning there are no more sounds
of scuttling.

I sweep the floors of the closets, clean
down to the boards.

2.

We've been here before. The loyalty of parents
when their kids perform. High school plays
can have their moments, between the slow, jerky
changes of scenes.

This time we don't recognize our son,
bent with the weight of eighty years,
voice older than my father's before he died.

It's not so much the wig, the fragile silver hair,

as it is the tremor in the voice, the hand.

We have read the novel, think we know
what we are in for.
But when our son repeats
to the ranch hands who want to kill his old dog,
"I've had him from a pup," and when
the dog is shot and David's back jerks,
when we see him an old man turning to the wall
in a narrow bed before an audience of hundreds,
I am gripped by something harsher than stage lights,
darker than the farthest corner of this auditorium
after everyone has gone home.

In the glare of the lobby, I can't find him
among the kids accepting hugs and flowers.
Can this be my son? I ask him
to pull off the wisps of beard, I have to touch
his neck, his cheek, I have to know
it is still his young skin
under that white hair.

Driving home without him, we don't talk,
I lean on you the way I used to.
We thought we knew what we were in for.
We used to quote from Steinbeck's novel: I would say
"Tell me about the rabbits," and you would read
from Rodale's *Raising Small Livestock*.
You said we would build the cages
so the rabbits could be kept clean, dry,
well-fed, could tend their young.

3.

That fall morning we found
David out by the pool kneeling
over the edge, over a field mouse
he was lifting from the hose that floats on the water.
The mouse must have fallen in during the night,
must have swum to the hose and clung
until our son woke
to find him trembling.

We dried his fur with a garden glove,
carried him to a hollow in the grasses, brought
bird seed from the house, and left him alone.

At first when we went to check, he was still there.
But later, when we went again, there was only
the wind sweeping the grass.

Generation

The eggs that have dropped alone into the womb
over the years, hundreds
of millions of sperm that have shrivelled
in their struggle up through the soft plush
to reach the great sun, ovum, be the one
who makes the successful stab at the vast arc,
pierces the envelope.
                    And the ovum, embracing
the one who finds her, the sleek
one who pillows himself so surprisingly
determined under her covers, this tiny whipping
pulse that plunges upriver
to reach her or die, she is so moved
she lets him
break her tight closed circle,
wave and rock through her entirety
until she finds herself multiplied, two
in one, four of two, eight from four,
till a face takes shape, fingers
separate from the palm of a hand
that assumes a shape like the hand of
the woman who surrounds all this,
who thinks she has caused all this
while a hand strokes her abdomen, her hand
pulls him down to her again
                    and again not thinking
of all the eggs yet stored
that will never be opened, never have
the chance to lose
whatever it was they had been.

At 50, Choosing New Makeup

The world asks, how are you, and I never know
what to say. A word, a phrase won't do it.
Cosmetics at the counter—bottles, tubes, liquids
to cover the face. Ivory Beige. Tawny Glow. Porcelain Rose.
I could say, I'm fine, I'm Ivory Beige.

Eye makeup I gave up long ago.
The times I used to cry and the mascara
ran black, even when the label said *Light
Brown*, tunnels staining my cheeks.
Pain of not knowing who I was.

Shopping for skins can drive you wild.
How much does the world need to know?
When my father died I wore the first pink I ever owned.
The folds of the skirt hung in the closet like an azalea, new lips
opening among the dark flannels and tweeds.

If I could decide on one of these shades, cover
the red clusters, broken vessels of my face.
I have found my breathing spaces.
How it feels to look you straight on skin to skin.
This business of artifice

when the ache to connect drives
deeper than it ever did at twenty, the tide rushes
swifter than anyone told you it could. On my hand
veins rise, blue as water from a distance. Rivers
through the body, all that has passed and passed by.

In Venice the Travelers

lighten, they have left behind
London, rectangular landmarks,
neighborhoods of the famous

novelists, upholstered homes
of Dickens, Carlyle. Have left
the clacking of their jet-lagged heels

dragging through Bloomsbury, through
the floors of the National Portrait
Gallery, lines of public faces.

Ready for Venice, for water
that lures them over bridges
whose names they can't pronounce,

lures them into shops glistening
with glass swirled into vines, petals, swans
shimmering like the canals

that dazzle silver flowers in the afternoon,
the water that blazes, crackles gold
blood loosed to the tide

in the evening. When they stop, catch
their breath, they stare down into the chasm
lengthening shadow that shapes

the under arch of a bridge
and their eyes fix on the water
beneath. Nothing is reflected.

They no longer remember
what they had forgotten to tell
the neighbor who is watching the house,

no longer notice who stands next to them
on the bridge, or the moment
they let drop with no splash

their memory of maps,
the way to go back,
the shapes of their own faces.

Inheritance

After my father died, my mother talked of a tree
she had seen at the edge of a field in fall:
a great tree as if on fire, she said, and she wanted
the rest of her life to be like that, one blaze
before the leaves fell, before it all was gone.
Now in the entry near her front door hangs a print
of a winter tree, rounded, heavy, white with snow.

Late winter, you and I have walked this way so often.
I thought I knew what to expect, oaks dropping
their brittle leaves, pushed off by their own buds.
Juniper, scrub. Grasses bent, shadowed with mold.

There is never a way to describe the things that rise
before you. A flush of white straight ahead, a breath
lifting. We turn from the path we'd been following,
into the mud of an abandoned road, to face this scent
of blossom, these circling bees, this bursting:
an old pear, gone back to its wild, original rootstock,
blooming over its intricate branches, a perfect oval.

WAY OF WHITENESS

. . . until the whole field is a
white desire, empty, a single stem,
a cluster, flower by flower,
a pious wish to whiteness gone over. . . .
                                    —W. C. Williams

All month the moths hovered,
bits and slaps of white pricking
the green mist: yarrow
at Fountains Abbey, dotted blossoms
clustered among leaves and branches, the white
rumps of lazing goats on the hills,
two white horses, muscles
grazing moorland above the Haworth parsonage.

This summer I have been tracking whiteness.
Clusters like doilies, caps, crowns,
but away from our own country
we aren't sure of the names.

You said elderberry, it could have been Queen Anne's lace.
And on the train the row after row of windows,
one after the other, rhythm of lines
of trees bordering fields, furrows.

The colors friends wore changed daily,
jackets of jade and pink, yellow, green, brilliant
as the crème de menthe at one time
I had thought a fancy drink.

Until this trip I had never had time to walk
behind Chartres, to stop and face the row
of white blooming trees, hawthorns, I finally decided,
masses of white clustering sweet flowers.
Tree after tree, each one almost
as tall as the cathedral.

In Strasbourg on the river blackening one night
someone spotted a swan and suddenly
there were dozens gathered in a cove
of the river, a progression of white neck after
white sliding into the dark.

Miracle of sweet milk in coffee.
Dissolving.
Until, finally at Canterbury, there was only this: white
clouds sweeping behind a spire, the spire
easing into the white
sky filling vision.

And this was even before the music
filled the interior spaces
of the choir at Evensong.

from **LET THE ICE SPEAK** (1991)

Baptism

Light dim as the crumbled leather
of old books, and Granny next to me
leaning down with her smell of lime cologne,
finger moving across the small black shapes.
She pointed to the clusters in their tidy lines,
barely stopping under each one, as the minister
kept on talking. My baby sister slept
as he held her, no one else
seemed to breathe.
                    But Granny's finger led
my eyes on and on, back and forth, down the page,
and then I saw: she reached *the* at the same time
the minister said *the,* and it happened again,
two lines down, and there were *the's* everywhere
on those pages—"even unto *the* end of *the* world,"
her finger moved as he said the words
out loud, "*the* kingdom, and *the* power,
and *the* glory," naming.

My Father's Living Room

Evening papers
crinkled in his lap,
his hands were clean,
nails trimmed short, his signet ring
had no initial.
I read the headlines from the floor,
trying to see inside, squinting to read
the little letters under the thick ones.
He turned the pages slowly.

"Don't bother your father," my mother
whispered. I learned not to. I practiced
quiet, practiced over and over
scales of silences,
learning as long as I didn't
startle him,
I could make my move
when the paper came down.

As we talked I would shiver
from holding in my words,
from not letting them out
too loudly,
from holding my ribs
close as piano keys
so I could sound
his fears.

Playing the Game of Statues

Whirling and whirling as the Tucson sun
curled down, we turned so dizzy
the purple mountains would set
firm in a wide stripe dividing the haze
of gray roofs from red sky
until, having spun ourselves
out of orbit like spent tops,
we fell frozen until the one who was It
gave orders, told us to *move*.
And move we did, a frenzy of leaping,
skating, arcing our backs for the high
dive and then letting go, over and over,
to land—*stop*—on the high wire
right there on the Bermuda grass
beneath our bare feet.
                             At the Galleria
dell'Accademia in Firenze, Michelangelo's
Four Slaves are still trying to separate
sinewy arms from the bulk of marble.
The David appears at the precise moment
he has become who he will be,
his head turned to one side, while we
circle around him, circle and stare
at such polished stasis, at the perfect
veins of his ankles.

How the rest of the body follows
the crisis of an instant—a freak pose
on an Arizona night
when the clouds boiled in the colors
of the High Renaissance Masters

and we whirled and flew and tried on other lives,
pirouetting or pitching, tight-rope-walking
for all we were worth,
still believing that, whenever you wanted,
you could always change your mind.

Dancing Lessons

A white shirt pressed his shoulders
as he taught me how to let my hand rest
in his. "A good dancer
never feels heavy in her partner's
arms," he said, so I worked
at keeping my palm a little distant

while my father's arm held my back.
"You must anticipate your partner's
next move, he should feel as if you're part
of him, always let him lead," he advised
as he dipped and toed, looking off
somewhere beyond my head.

I stumbled backward around the room
trying to keep in line
with the tidy circles he made
avoiding the green chair,
the converted player piano, my sisters' toys.
I didn't mind the music, Cole Porter was okay.

But I could feel my sweat steaming
like the dishwater my mother stood over,
her red wool shirt
above the suds, the clatter.
And as the silver jangled
offbeat in the drainer

I dreamed of climbing up to the roof.
Might be hard to dance on sloped shingles,
but there'd be night air,
maybe a breeze, my body could breathe.

Black Sheep, White Stars

He'd appear like a bird
that wanders into a place
on its way between two continents.
Surrounded by houses
that sopped up sparkle like sponges
he'd roll out of a '47 black Cadillac

and wave a bottle of rum
shimmering in the sun like amber.
"Pam, darling," he'd call to my mother,
his voice so raucous
Mrs. Simonitch next door
would move one slat of her Venetian blinds.

His toes pushed from limp *huaraches*
and he grinned as if he knew
just how much acid
the sight of him
shadow-bearded, yellow under the arms,
produced in my father's stomach.

When he talked
our windows grew arches, opened doors
onto courtyards, lemon trees, parrots,
we could hear the rustling of green feathers,
the chirrings and cawings of orange birds.
Small on the sofa I said

"Let me come live with you,"
something in my lungs knowing
that in a place named Tlayacapan
people might swallow drinks

the colors of bougainvillea
and move at night

to music that had never heard
of a metronome.
And when Uncle Dick and his friend Pedro
sat me between them
on the Cadillac's dusty front seat
to watch *High Society* at the Frontier Drive In,

I held myself taut and sweaty, dreaming stars
thicker than sugar on oatmeal,
stars farther than heaven,
stars and hibiscus and mangoes
that could cluster around a life
as long as a laugh.

Why We Went to the Ocean

That screen door slammed on too much silence.
In the car we carried it with us.
It was Daddy who muttered and fussed
about the luggage, but only to Mom
when we weren't around, so all we knew
were the great sighs, my mother's solicitous
gestures, suggestions for where to fit
the big brown bag, the box with the extra towels.
He would never be able to get it all in.

My mother kept us quiet,
hissing to the back seat.
He needed quiet to drive. The roads
were harder then, two lanes, tricky
to pass, to keep your own speed.
The heat blew in from the windows,
mixed with our father's smoke, the smoke
from the Benson & Hedges that thickened
and stopped the air.

The desert stuck in my eyes
a great brown thorny silence
until we climbed up the mountains
before San Diego and the green
began its small damp murmurings.
We could stop for lunch, walk
around, find pine needles bundled
like tiny brooms, like the wire
brushes drummers use.

From then on the roads were wider.

From then on we stretched as tall as we could
from the back seat, waiting for that first
glimpse of the long breath
of blue stretching out beyond
the horizon, and it was downhill then,
as we sang out *the sea, the sea,*
and there it was, we could run
along its slapping hard breathing
body, we could laugh as loud as we
ever wanted because the ocean
had the loudest voice in the whole world.

Once More, Squam Lake

The lake whitens in the hot light
of July. At Sandy Beach we see the sunfish
circling their eggs, rippling the water.
The sunfish do what they've done before,
will do again. I sit in a haze

of sisters, nieces, mothers, grandmothers.
When I was seven, Old Jane Noble was Young
Jane Noble. When I was seventeen
she was one of the mothers who knitted
argyles on the playhouse porch.

Too hot today for socks, for knitting.
But tonight the loons will yodel
and last week they counted
nine new chicks, three more than last year.
My son is learning to fish the lake.

My father will teach him
to let the line fall quietly
(only a small furrow of water moving
beyond the nylon thread),
to hear where bass live, to find the depth

of the lake. I watch from the dock,
the lake takes the planks and rocks them
backward, forward, I forget
how old I am, what year it is,
how it all matters.

Father's Fish

I have seen them flop and heave
silver muscle on the boat bottom
and these were not those fish.

Rather they were feathers,
amethysts, sunsets,
clouds swirling and gleaming

in a rectangular blue world
he kept perfect: temperature,
pH, plants, clean gravel, all

perfect. And silent. Such brilliant
silences. Even the mouths
of the neon tetras, of the knife-narrow

black and white triangular angels
opened only the way a cry
in a dream clutches at silence,

the throat tries, strains
to be heard, aches to reach
the ears that stand

on the other side of the glass
but there is no sound, nothing.
And perhaps the ears would rather

watch, only follow with the eyes
the fishy sliverings, the tailings
and questionings round and round

in the water, and forget what it took
to keep it all going: emptying
the tubes, cleaning the white

gravel, replacing the charcoal,
never overfeeding. It may have been
too much trouble.

There is no longer an aquarium
in that house. Now
on a Northern lake I see him

bent in the boat, hands
trembling as he changes
the lure, prepares

to cast over
the lake's blue ridges,
hoping to reach

the mouths of small bass
as they shimmer
under dark rocks, cut

through dark water,
hoping their mouths
will open eye to eye with his,

yet knowing
that the only way

it will happen

will come in the sharp pull
they both hear,
silent, when the hook holds.

Requiscat, For My Father

1.
No more travel
on this lake for now.
His boat has been stored and soon
the ice will begin to gather.
In the heaviest month
the men will come to cut the ice.
Great cubes. Lift them into the icehouse,
pile on pile, up to the roof.
Somewhere off Loon Island
his bones have been scattered.
Ashes, they call them, but
I know better. They will take a long time
to melt.

2.
Summer evenings on the screened porch,
breeze in the pines, clinking
of ice and sweet smell
of Scotch from their glasses
while we sipped
ginger ale, tried not to argue,
allowed to sit with the grownups.
I had white socks, blue barrettes
clipped over my braids
and was beginning to know
how hungry I was
for dinner.

It will be a long time
before I can hear

the jingle of ice in a glass.
I avoid groups, political
discussions, people who say
they've never been better.

3.
How many pieces of line left
at the bottom of the lake? Hooks
caught on rocks, lures
lost in the sand. And the last
great catch, eight four-pounders
he caught with Sam Howe,
a day in heaven they said,
until they found
that neither had secured
the stringer, the whole day's catch
gone back to the lake.
No story had ever been quite so funny,
and yet they had lost
the catch of their lives,
and it was my father's last.
But they'd had the day, he said.

All those soft places
under the lake, places he had only
found in the last few years,
his hair thin, silvery as the scales
of the small-mouthed bass
he had begun to learn
to bring up into the boat.
It tired him to clean them

down on the dock,
stooping over, but he wanted
to cook them for dinner.

4.
The ice is patching the lake
together, even now as I watch
cool shadows thread the fields.
We will leave the sandy bottom
alone for awhile, the tenderness
of moss on rocks.

Let the ice crust.
By June, when we take the metal pick
to the chunk of blue ice
cut from the lake and stored
under layers of clean straw
we will turn and face
the wide water that stretches
to Red Hill, to East
and West Rattlesnake Mountains,
and we will let the ice speak,
let the ice speak in the glass.

from **WINTER CHICKENS** (1990)

Winter Chickens

Not sure if the clucking is child's crying—
sometimes the sound winds out
through walls of wire mesh,
orange rinds, saturated leaves.
Red wattles hang from their heads,
eggs squirm from swollen vents,
still damp slick
and amazing as Meissen china.
Carry them inside

for the transformation:
eggs into water,
poached ovals on toast,
eggs in bowls before stirring to scramble,
eggs tossed in a smoking pan
sliding around like shoes on mud.
The shells go back to the hens,
grit for their old, hard beaks.

The Navy Blue Chair

Wraps quiet in its smooth chintz,
silent as a rabbit,
as the black dazzle of midnight.

Outside the kitchen a phoebe
sits on three eggs
while I rinse the omelet pan.

The chair's fabric
is slick as an egg, the chair
knows nothing of bloodshed.

Has no need for language.
Only there is something
in the easy curve

of the firm high back
that might allow anything, anything
at all: hatching, feathering,

rising through dark air
with the lift of a Mozart sonata
the lilt of a perfect soufflé.

After the dishes are finished
I want to sit down. If I sit
long enough in the blue chair

I may know when the phoebe's young
will crack through to the air,
when the summer storms will break—

when the clashing of flesh and beak,
the loud pounding of hard rain,
of hard flight,

will have to begin.

Schönbrunn Yellow

The summer palace of the Hapsburgs is yellow
and inside, gilt climbs the walls like ivy.

Maria Theresa had sixteen children in this house.
To keep them she had 400 maids.

The yellow walls are the color
of the woman's apron in Brueghel's painting,

a woman dancing on village dirt,
dancing in an apron thick with grease,

an apron hard with scraps of dough.
Maria Theresa's favorite painting

was of three peasants, a family taking a walk in the hills,
a family of peasants like Brueghel's, dancing

and drinking, filling their cheeks with cereal
and beer the color of gold.

Night Song

The room lies vague
beyond the glare of the Tensor lamp.
Two circles of light cluster like daisies
in the blackness beyond the window:

one's a neighbor's porch light, one's down
farther, by the road.
The darkness hums even-paced
under your snores irregular as a dripping tap,

jagged as thunder.
What is there to see in a dark house?
Refrigerator whirring and clicking,
two cars going past, one right after the other.

More for the ears than the eyes.
The dog shifts in his sleep, bumps the door,
our child rustles in his blankets.
Only the old hamster

creeps over to his plastic wheel
and starts the nightly run
on his red wheel
through Siberian fields of grain

that toss and quiver as quietly,
as edibly, as sleep.

Swallow Watcher

Every house needs someone to watch the swallows,
someone willing
to half close the eyes, lean the head back
against a tall chair
in a garden, on a porch, in a courtyard.

It doesn't matter if a cheap paperback
falls wrinkled from the knees,
a wine glass dangles
empty from the hand.
What matters is the watching:
                                        following

the lifts and darts
of the small birds,
the racings and screechings over territory,
the jags and dips for insects,
the gliding on wind.

About the time
the neighbor's porch light comes on
and the sky
can't hold color any more
the swallow watcher moves inside

to the glare of living room lights,
but he turns, leans
against the cool glass of the sliding door,
and stares out at the dark sifting down,
quiet as feathers, as wings.

Coming through December

The rooms were no longer
ours, had lost definition.

Visitors do that. Their
needs turn floors into shapes

neither yours nor theirs,
spaces become no space.

Crowded kitchen, hard work
just talking, listening,

making your way
to the coffee,

table littered with crayons
and plastic teething rings.

The linings of the house
begin to sag, tear. I turn

from room to room, ask you
"Will it be all right?"

At night I wander through rooms
filled with sounds of sleeping

and stroke my hands over the walls,
rubbing smooth the names of the spaces:

kitchen, a room for one orange,

a black-handled knife,

and sunlight; *study*,
a place for each word cut perfectly

shaped with its colors and fiber
peppery, tart, intact.

Everyone gone but one sister,
and we go down to the coast

for the whooping cranes
that fly 2000 miles

to these tidelands
where the eye doesn't stop, keeps going

over watery grass and tide,
marshland both river and sea,

fresh and salt, neither one thing
nor the other. Water and sky

the same gray. Reeds and leaves
the same brown. Herons hunch so silent

the bank seems part of their wings,
grassy feathers. Over the wetlands

the cranes rise
tall as grown children.

Their necks curve like snow
lining the arc of an oak trunk

as they break acorn snails,
blue crabs in their beaks,

shell
and weed glistening.

∞

Driving back to town
the world is divided in two:

navy earth and orange sky
and we are hungry.

We order oysters, they are hot
fried, so fresh their white flesh

glows blue. We talk about the snow geese
we had just passed, swooping

down to the black field by the road,
the water in the furrows

gleaming across the mud.
We say how there were hundreds

of geese clacking, lining
the field, quieting

as the dark
brought two worlds into one.

∞

When a crane pulls one leg

from the water,

the leg shines a slim black line
on the yellow grasses.

Poised, the leg at that moment
belongs to the crane

until it pushes forward, down
again, toward the next bite of snail.

Back now in the house
from the market, I carry

the silence of white cranes
through every one of these rooms,

burnish them
silver and blue, salty,

fresh, from the long
pools of origin.

ACKNOWLEDGMENTS

I am extremely grateful to the editors of the following magazines and collections, in which some of these poems earlier appeared, at times in different versions.

NEW POEMS

Alaska Quarterly Review	"Not Montale's Eel"
Aperçus	"In the Galápagos," "After the Shooting in Tucson"
Cold Mountain Review	"About Chocolate"
Diode	"Circlings"
The Halcyone Literary Review	"Rilke to Roethke on Rosh Hashana"
The Kenyon Review	"Why Cages"
The Laurel Review	"In Praise of Stumps," "Sour Take"
Tar River Poetry	"On Stain Removal," "The Butterfly Return"
Plume	"On Salt"
Plume 9 Anthology	"On Delta Flght #2164 From JFK"
Poetry Bay	"That Bell for Ethel"
Poetry Northwest	"In Light of the Eclipse"
Prairie Schooner	"One Week After the Election," "The Dirt"
The Southern Review	"On Scissors and Matisse," "After Reading Baudelaire," "Lifted"
Upstreet	"Finding Mahogany in Belize"
Valparaiso Poetry Review	"In the Gallery"

GLOSS (Saint Julian Press, 2020):

Ilanot Review	"Ivory Carvings"
Plume	"Elegant, She Said," "Latent Image"
Prairie Schooner	"Surgery, A Little History"
The Southern Review	"What Surfaces," "Silk Roads," "Interior"
Superstition Review	"Gathering Bones"
Valparaiso Poetry Review	"Beyond a Certain Age, I Look for Paris in Paris"

"Gathering Bones" was reprinted in *Womens' Voices for Change*, poetry editor, Rebecca Foust, (http://women'svoicesforchange.org/tag/poetry-sunday).

"'Elegant,' She Said," was reprinted in *Nasty Women Poets*, edited by Grace Bauer and Julie Kane, Lost Horse Press.

SHIMMER (Glass Lyre Press, 2019)

Exit 7	"On the Chinese Scroll"
Journal of Compressed Creative Arts	"The Silver Tongs," "Even Tarnished"
Nimrod	"The Dragon Bowl"
Poetry Bay	"Along a River," "Maybe His Boat," "How a Surface"

From ONE BLACKBIRD AT A TIME (BkMk Press, Winner of the John Ciardi Prize, 2015)

Cerise Press	"Waking Over Call It Sleep"
Connecticut Review	"Arriving at Wallace Stevens in the 13th Week"
Diode	"Langston Hughes' 'Weary Blues'"
Paterson Literary Review	"About That 'One Art'"

The Southern Review	"Books, Bath Towels, and Beyond," "I Hate Telling People I Teach English," "Truth, Beauty, and the Intro Poetry Workshop," "Teaching *Mrs. Dalloway* I'm Thinking," "The Last Time I Taught Robert Frost"

"Books, Bath Towels, and Beyond," is included in *The Best American Poetry* 2013, eds. Denise Duhamel and David Lehman (Scribner).

"Teaching *Mrs. Dalloway* I'm Thinking" was reprinted on *Verse Daily,* www.versedaily.org.

FROM THE MOON THE EARTH IS BLUE (Wings Press, 2015):

American Literary Review	"Apology for Blue"
The Journal	"Composition in Gray"
Southern Poetry Review	"Apologia for Brown"

The Blanton Museum, http://blantonmuseum.org/experience_the_blanton_poetry_project.cfm. "High Yellow"

From NOTHING BETWEEN US (Del Sol Press, 2009)

New York Quarterly	"Freed Up"
Ontario Review	"Audio Visual," "Half and Half," "Remedial Reading," "Teaching *Uncle Tom's Children*"

Suddenly: An Anthology of Sudden Fiction and Prose Poetry, IV

"Macramé"

From THINGS OF THE WEATHER (Pudding House, 2008)

Blue Mesa Review	"Contrails," "Stratus Opacus Nebulosus"
Poetry	"Thunder," "Cumulus and Cirrus"

"Cumulonimbus Incus" and "Cumulus and Cirrus" also appeared online in *Poetry Daily*

From **BETWEEN FRAMES** (Pecan Grove Press, 2006)

Concho River Review   "Trash"

"Trash" also appeared in *Falling from Grace in Texas: A Literary Response to the Demise of Paradise*, edited by Rick Bass and Paul Christensen (Wings Press).

From **POEMS FROM PARADISE** (WordTech, 2005)

Poet Lore   "Lemon, Oak, Cypress"

Poetry Kanto   "The Third Week"

From **WAY OF WHITENESS** (Wings Press, 2000)

The American Scholar   "*Of Mice and Men*"

The Antioch Review   "In Venice the Travellers"

Borderlands   "Inheritance"

The Journal   "Way of Whiteness"

Poetry   "Taking a Language"

River Sedge   "Some Days the Only"

Spoon River Poetry Review   "Liquid Poem"

Tar River Poetry   "The Bottom"

From **LET THE ICE SPEAK** (Ithaca House, 1991)

The American Scholar   "Requiescat, for My Father"

California Quarterly   "Playing the Game of Statues"

Concho River Review   "Baptism"

Crosscurrents   "Why We Went to the Ocean"

Imagine: International Chicano Poetry Journal

                    "Dancing Lessons"

Nimrod   "Father' Fish"

Passages North   "Once More, Squam Lake"

Poetry   "Black Sheep, White Stars"

From **WINTER CHICKENS** (Corona Publishing, 1990)

The American Scholar   "Schönbrunn Yellow,"
                                    "Swallow Watcher"

New America   "Winter Chickens"

Nimrod   "Coming Through

Poetry   "The Navy Blue Chair,"
                                    "Night Song"

"Swallow Watcher" appeared in *Anthology of Magazine Verse & Yearbook of American Poetry, 1986-1988*, edited by Alan F. Pater.

Without the help of friends along the way, these poems could never have been written. First and foremost, Sandra M. Gilbert provided loving encouragement and advice from the very beginning, when, in 1975, I tremblingly took to her office at UC Davis, where I was starting work on my Ph.D., a draft of this little poem:

PRACTICE

Honing   I'm
Sharpening   my
Knives   for
Cutting   cleaving through
Greenpeppers   opening their
Halves   crackle moist
Dark   white feathers tiny
Seeds   clinging.
This green

meat   will make

good eating   I

will swallow   the seeds

and grow   wings.

("Practice" was later included in *Poems' Progress,* Absey & Co.)

Sandra was amazingly supportive. She urged me to submit to the *California Quarterly,* and the editors even accepted "Practice." I took every poetry workshop Sandra offered. She generously and brilliantly commented on all the poems I drafted until I moved from California to San Antonio to begin teaching at UT San Antonio. It was in Sandra's workshops that I met my gifted long-time poetry buddy, Kevin Clark. It was also in one of Sandra's workshops that I met Alicia Ostriker, who had visited our class before giving a reading that night, whose presence dazzled me and who has been a generous support and inspiration ever since.

Along the way, so many kindly ones have helped with poems. My former husband, Laurence Barker, read and responded to all my early poems. Other members of my support system have included Sharon Ankrum, Vera Banner, Kacee Belcher, David Dooley, Cyra Dumitru, Michele Flom, Sarah Grieve, Sue Hum, Paulette Jiles, Jacqueline Kolosov, Doran Larson, Christine Dumaine Leche, David Dodd Lee, Terry Lucas, Bonnie Lyons, Sherry McKinney, Pat Mora, Naomi Shihab Nye, Alberto Ríos, Sudeep Sen, Melissa Shepherd, Amritjit Singh, Veda Smith, Darrell Stafford, David Ray Vance, and Diane Wakoski. And I still grieve the loss of three other precious friends, all valuable writers and critics: Catherine Kasper, Jeannine Keenan, and Barbara Stanush, each of whom left this life before we were ready. I still miss the wit and wisdom of Ruth Stone, whose example and encouragement were pivotal for years.

I continue to be thankful for our nourishing San Antonio poetry group that includes my precious long-time friend and wonderful writer Natalia Treviño, along with the terrific poets Joshua Robbins, Stephanie

Schoellman, and Alexandra Van de Kamp. And my graduate students often provide excellent, helpful reactions.

For years, Hannah Stein and Kevin were the editors upon whom I most relied. These days, it's also Ralph Black, Alice Friman, Joel Peckham, Barbara Ras, and, of course, Kevin, without whom I doubt I could ever "finish" a poem.

And my generous, brilliant husband Steven G. Kellman "signs off" on every draft before I ever submit a page to a journal. For his keen critical eye and and ear I am more grateful than I can say.

I must also profusely thank Ben Furnish of BkMk Press for his encouragement and expertise.

I offer reams of thanks for the support of my amazing sisters, Patricia McConnell and Liza Piatt.

And the understanding of my beloved son David Barker means worlds beyond worlds to me.

Wendy Barker's seventh full-length collection of poetry is *Gloss,* published by Saint Julian Press in 2020. Her collection *One Blackbird at a Time* was chosen for the John Ciardi Prize and was published by BkMk Press in 2015. Earlier books include her novel in prose poems, *Nothing Between Us: The Berkeley Years* (runner-up for the Del Sol Prize and released by Del Sol Press in 2009); *Poems from Paradise* (WordTech, 2005); *Way of Whiteness* (Wings Press, 2000); *Let the Ice Speak* (Ithaca House, 1991); and *Winter Chickens* (Corona Publishing Co., 1990).

Over Roads, Under Moons (Alabrava Press, 2022) is Wendy's sixth chapbook. Her fifth chapbook, *Shimmer,* was published in 2019 by Glass Lyre Press, and a fourth chapbook, *From the Moon, Earth is Blue,* was published in 2015, by Wings Press. Earlier chapbooks include *Things of the Weather* (Pudding House Press, 2009); *Between Frames* (Pecan Grove Press, 2006); and *Eve Remembers* (Aark Arts, 1996). An anthology, *Far Out: Poems of the 60s,* co-edited with David M. Parsons, was published in 2016 by Wings Press. A selection of poems accompanied by autobiographical essays, *Poems' Progress* (Absey & Co.), appeared in 2002, and a collection of translations (with Saranindranath Tagore) from the Bengali of India's Nobel Prize-winning poet, *Rabindranath Tagore: Final Poems* (George Braziller, 2001), received the Sourette Diehl Fraser Award from the Texas Institute of Letters.

Wendy's poems and translations have appeared in hundreds of journals, including *Poetry, The Southern Review, The Georgia Review, The Gettysburg Review, Plume, Rattle, The American Scholar, The Kenyon Review, Nimrod, Stand, Partisan Review, Michigan Quarterly Review, Plume, New Letters, Antioch* and *Southern Poetry Review.* Her work has also appeared in numerous anthologies, including *The Best American Poetry 2013* (eds. Denise Duhamel and David Lehman). Many poems have been reprinted in various venues, including the Academy of American Poets site poets.org. Essays have appeared in such magazines as *Poets & Writers* and *Southwest Review.* She has read her poetry at dozens of universities, bookstores, festivals, and conferences in the United States, Europe, and in India.

As a scholar, she is the author of *Lunacy of Light: Emily Dickinson and the Experience of Metaphor* (Southern Illinois University Press, 1987) as well as co-editor (with Sandra M. Gilbert) of *The House is Made of Poetry: The Art of Ruth Stone* (Southern Illinois University Press, 1996).

Recipient of an NEA fellowship, a Rockefeller residency fellowship in Bellagio, as well as other awards in poetry, including the Writers' League of Texas Book Award (which she has received twice, for *Way of Whiteness* in 2000 and for *Between Frames* in 2007) and the Mary Elinore Smith Poetry Prize from *The American Scholar*, she has also been a Fulbright senior lecturer in Bulgaria. Her work has been translated into Hindi, Chinese, Japanese, Russian, and Bulgarian. Poet-in-Residence and the Pearl Lewinn Endowed Chair at the University of Texas at San Antonio, where she has taught since 1982, Wendy is married to the critic, biographer, and poet Steven G. Kellman.

BkMk Press began celebrating its fiftieth anniversary in 2021. After thirty-eight years at the University of Missouri-Kansas City, BkMk returned to being an independent press in 2021. is grateful for the support it has recently received in recent years from the following organizations and individuals:

Missouri Arts Council
Miller-Mellor Foundation
Neptune Foundation
Richard J. Stern Foundation for the Arts
Stanley H. Durwood Foundation
William T. Kemper Foundation

Anonymous
Dwight Arn
Beverly Burch
Jaimee Wriston Colbert
Maija Rhee Devine
Ben Furnish
Charles Egan
Alice Friman
Anna Jaffe & Michael Horine
Michael Jaffe
Tamar Jaffe and Mike Reyes
Whitney and Mariella Kerr
Carla Klausner
Lorraine M. López
Patricia Cleary Miller
Margot Patterson
Peppermint Creek Theatre Company
Elizabeth Goldring Piene
Alan Proctor
James Hugo Rifenbark
Sylvia Stuckey
Roderick and Wyatt Townley